Dedication

My late grandfather, ***Shree Girja Shankar Dubey.***

Passive Income 2024

A Practical Guide

Ignite Brilliance, Craft Prosperity,
Connect Powerfully...

AMIT DUBEY | NAINA SANDHIR

INDIA · SINGAPORE · MALAYSIA

ISBN 979-8-89233-473-0

Contents

Preface

Dear Reader,

In the labyrinth of opportunities that life presents, there's a hidden gem waiting to be uncovered, and it's within your grasp. This book is not just a guide; it's an invitation to transform your perspective, embrace new possibilities, and chart a course toward financial freedom. Allow me to share the essence of why I write and what awaits you in the pages ahead.

I write for you – the aspiring professional, the student with dreams, the freelancer seeking autonomy, the founder navigating the entrepreneurial journey, the sales professional aiming for new heights, the job seeker navigating the competitive landscape, the nonprofit professional making a difference, and all those hungry for passive income and networking opportunities on the powerful professional platform that is LinkedIn.

Why do I write? In the context of the United Nations' Sustainable Development Goals, with "No Poverty" leading the charge in 2024, this book emerges as a beacon to dismantle the shackles of the "Poverty mindset." Billions of working professionals, students, freelancers, founders, and job seekers either underutilize LinkedIn or remain unaware of its transformative capabilities. This book is my initiative to empower you, to shift your mindset from a passive observer to an active participant in the realm of passive income and networking.

So, what will you achieve after immersing yourself in these pages? Beyond the practical strategies and actionable insights, you will embark on a journey of awareness, realization, and transformation—the ART's fundamental work. You'll become aware of the powerful networking platform and income streams waiting at your fingertips. Realization will dawn as you recognize your innate potential to thrive in this digital landscape. This newfound awareness and realization will lead to a profound Transformation, where consistent actions pave the way for a passive income stream and a network that propels you toward success.

How does this impact your life? Picture a life where new income streams work diligently to build wealth for you. Envision a LinkedIn profile not just as a virtual resume but as a dynamic force field that attracts opportunities. This book has the power to reshape not only your mindset but also your reality.

In conclusion, this isn't just a book—it's your ticket to a realm where the potential of LinkedIn is harnessed for your benefit. It's an opportunity to break free from the constraints of a poverty mindset and embrace a future where financial freedom and networking prowess are within reach.

Are you ready to transform your LinkedIn journey? Turn the page and embark on a voyage where possibilities unfold, and your dreams become not just aspirations but tangible realities.

With anticipation,

Amit Dubey

Acknowledgment

In the pursuit of penning my very first book, I've been immensely blessed and inspired by an incredible circle of support that has uplifted me every step of the way. Expressing gratitude feels like whispering a heartfelt thank you amidst the stars, each twinkle representing an integral part of my journey.

To the pillar of strength in my life, my late grandfather, Shree Girja Shankar Dubey—your legacy of wisdom and encouragement continues to illuminate my path, guiding my endeavors even now.

In the embrace of my nurturing joint family, I owe immense thanks to my parents, Shree Omkar Nath Dubey and Sushma Dubey, my late uncle Shree Yogender Dubey, Aunt Upasna Dubey, and my younger brother Saransh Dubey, whose unwavering support has been my cornerstone.

Special gratitude extends to my maternal family, the rock that has always stood firm in support—blessings from Maternal grandfather Shree Hriday Shankar Upadhyay, elder Maternal uncle Shree Anil Upadhyay, and Younger Arvind Upadhyay.

To my beloved wife and best friend, Sugandha Gupta Dubey, and my supportive in-laws, Shree Yash Pal Gupta and Raman Gupta, your love and belief in my aspirations have been my constant inspiration.

Gratitude knows no bounds for the mentors who guided me through life's labyrinth: Shree Anupam Kumar Shukla, and Daniel O. Livvarcin, your mentorship has been an invaluable compass guiding me through life's uncharted territories.

To my idols, Shree Pardeep Pathak, Manju Pathak, and Manish Dave, your life's canvas painted with success and resilience have been my source of motivation and aspiration.

And to the eternal friends, the unwavering support system from childhood to a lifetime—late Jagjeet Singh, Neha Tiwari, Radhika Baidya, Dax Bamania, and Mayur Vyas—your companionship has filled my life with joyous memories and endless encouragement.

Each name etched in these lines represents a beacon of support and inspiration, a guardian angel cheering me on as I embarked on this literary endeavor. To you all, I offer my sincerest gratitude—your presence in my life has been nothing short of a blessing.

With heartfelt thanks,

Amit Dubey

Review

Authored by the visionary duo, Amit and Naina, this book is not just a read; it's an awakening to the latent opportunities that lie within LinkedIn, a platform many of us use yet seldom to its full potential.

What left me in awe was the meticulous breakdown of strategies and real-world examples that transformed LinkedIn from a mere professional networking site to a goldmine for passive income. The authors have done a remarkable job of demystifying digital networking and monetization dynamics. Their approach is pragmatic yet innovative, offering various techniques tailored for beginners and seasoned LinkedIn users.

Amit and Naina's expertise shines throughout the book, particularly in emphasizing the importance of building meaningful connections and leveraging them for sustainable income streams. The book is more than just a guide; it's a mentor in print, leading you through the intricacies of digital marketing, personal branding, and strategic networking.

One of the most striking aspects of "LinkedIn Passive Income 2024" is its forward-thinking approach. The strategies outlined are not just for immediate gains but for long-term success. This aspect resonates deeply with me as it aligns with the ever-evolving nature of the digital world.

Daniel O. Livvarcin, PhD

Founder and CEO, Vectors Group, Canada.

About Author

Amit Dubey, the author of "LinkedIn Passive Income 2024: A Practical Guide," is a highly experienced Business Development Consultant, Brand Marketer, Sales Coach, and Keynote Speaker. With over nine years in the industry, he has mentored over 500 individuals and entrepreneurs, guiding them to achieve their business goals, generate substantial revenue, and build strong credibility. Amit's expertise lies in developing the right mindset, understanding the nuances of business development, and providing strategic support. His exceptional performance has earned him several awards, and his passion for helping others is evident through his engaging keynote speeches and live sessions. Whether you need assistance with business development, LinkedIn growth, content creation, brand strategy, or planning your entrepreneurial journey, Amit Dubey's extensive experience and expertise make him the perfect collaborator to help you realize your business dreams and achieve holistic success.

About Co-Author

Naina, known as TheMillennialRumi, is a co-author of the book "LinkedIn Passive Income 2024: A Practical Guide." Her remarkable journey as a creative writer is marked by a series of professional endeavors that ultimately led her to discover her true calling, storytelling, and creative writing. A prolific writer, her work encompasses a published book of prose named Roopantaran and an ever-growing repertoire of literary delights on Medium and LinkedIn. She believes in creating art from the heart and is a true litterateur.

CHAPTER 1

Introduction: An Overview of the Niche in 2024

"LinkedIn: Turning dreams into dollars, 24/7-Amit Dubey."

Are you tired of the daily grind, constantly trading your time for money? Do you dream of earning while you sleep, sipping coffee on a beach somewhere, knowing your bank account is growing without you lifting a finger? Well, you're not alone. You're part of a growing wave of individuals seeking financial freedom and flexibility through the tantalizing realm of passive income. And in the bustling world of digital opportunities, one platform stands out as a beacon for those ready to embark on the journey: LinkedIn.

But what exactly is LinkedIn passive income? Let's break it down. It's the money you earn on LinkedIn without having to work actively for it. Picture this: sponsored content, affiliate marketing, and digital products – all working for you, even as you catch up on your beauty sleep. Once set up, these income streams continue to pour in, a steady flow of revenue while you're busy living life.

So, why is LinkedIn the promised land for passive income seekers in 2024? The numbers tell a compelling story. The LinkedIn user base has been steadily growing, and projections for 2024 indicate a continuation of this trend. That means an ever-expanding audience waiting to be tapped into for passive income opportunities. And where there's potential, a thriving landscape of business opportunities is waiting to be explored.

Businesses, big and small, have realized the goldmine that is LinkedIn for marketing and lead generation. This translates to countless niches and industries ripe for the picking regarding passive income. Whether you're a financial guru, marketing maven, or tech wizard, there's an audience on LinkedIn hungry for what you have to offer.

Now, who can benefit from LinkedIn passive income? The answer is refreshingly simple: just about anyone! Whether you're an entrepreneur seeking to diversify income streams, a content creator aiming to monetize your following, or a marketer hungry for lead generation – LinkedIn has a place for you at the passive income table.

But it's not just about the money. It's about the lifestyle. Picture a life where you're not chained to your desk, can travel, spend time with family, or simply indulge in leisure without worrying about bills. That's the promise of passive income on LinkedIn.

"We embark on this journey, let's also glimpse into the crystal ball and uncover some key trends poised to shape the LinkedIn landscape in 2024. Brace yourself for the ascendancy of video content, taking center stage for its unmatched engagement. Automation and outsourcing are set to play pivotal roles, thanks to an array of tools designed to streamline the process on LinkedIn.

By the end of this chapter, you'll be armed with the knowledge of LinkedIn's potential, why it's a goldmine waiting to be explored, who can benefit, and the key trends shaping its landscape in 2024. So, if you're ready to transform your LinkedIn profile into a powerhouse, keep reading!

Welcome to LinkedIn, the world's largest professional network with over 1 billion members across 200 countries and territories. Here, the vision is clear: create economic opportunity for every member of the global workforce. The mission is simple yet powerful: connect the world's professionals to make them more productive and successful.

Let's arm ourselves with some staggering statistics as we embark on this journey. LinkedIn boasts 36 offices worldwide, with over 19,400 employees across 30 cities. Available in 26 languages, the platform transcends borders and connects professionals globally.

The numbers speak volumes. With 1 billion members, 67 million companies, and 65 million business decision-makers on board, LinkedIn is not just a social network: it's a thriving ecosystem of opportunities. And the platform's revenue surpassing $15 billion in Q4 FY23 attests to its undeniable success.

Whether you're submitting a job application (140 per second, to be precise), utilizing skills data for hiring (50% of hirers on LinkedIn do), or exploring new job opportunities (61 million users each week), LinkedIn is the go-to hub for professionals worldwide.

So, here's the deal: LinkedIn is not just a platform; it's a community of possibilities, a place where professionals gather to connect, stay informed, advance their careers, and work smarter. As we unravel the potential of LinkedIn passive income, remember you're not just joining a platform but becoming part of a global movement toward financial freedom and flexibility.

Now, let's dive deep into the world of LinkedIn passive income, where your dreams of earning while you sleep can become a reality.

Next Chapter: Building a Strong LinkedIn Profile

Chapter 2

Building a Strong LinkedIn Profile

If you're serious about generating passive income from LinkedIn, building a strong profile showcasing your skills and expertise is the first step. Simply said, you have it; you flaunt it! Your LinkedIn profile serves as your online resume and is often the first thing potential clients or customers will see when they come across your profile. Therefore, you must make an excellent first impression.

In this chapter, I'll provide a step-by-step guide to building a strong LinkedIn profile to attract potential passive income opportunities.

Step 1: Optimize Your Headline, Profile Picture, and Banner Image

Why Optimize Your LinkedIn Profile for Passive Income?

LinkedIn has emerged as the go-to platform for professionals and businesses to connect, network, and explore lucrative opportunities in today's digital era. With over **1 billion members worldwide,** LinkedIn offers immense potential for generating passive income. However, simply having a presence on LinkedIn is not enough. Optimizing your LinkedIn profile is crucial to maximize your chances of attracting passive income opportunities.

By optimizing your LinkedIn profile, you can:

1. **Enhance your professional branding:** Your LinkedIn profile acts as a personal branding tool, allowing you to showcase your expertise, skills, and accomplishments. A well-optimized profile creates a positive impression on potential passive income sources, positioning you as a credible and competent professional.
2. **Increase visibility and reach:** An optimized LinkedIn profile increases your visibility within the platform's vast user base. This heightened visibility enables you to attract the attention of individuals and organizations seeking professionals like yourself for passive income collaborations.
3. **Leverage the power of personalization:** LinkedIn offers several search and recommendation features that utilize keywords and profile information to match professionals with relevant opportunities. By optimizing your profile, you make it easier for LinkedIn's algorithm to identify you as a potential candidate for passive income ventures.

What to Consider When Optimizing Your LinkedIn Profile?

When optimizing your LinkedIn profile to attract passive income opportunities, consider the following key elements: your headline, profile picture, and banner photo.

Headline:

Your headline is the short phrase that appears right below your name on LinkedIn. Crafting a compelling headline that clearly conveys your professional expertise and the value you offer is crucial. Instead of using generic terms like "Job Seeker" or "Unemployed," focus on keywords relevant to your industry and skills. For example, a digital marketing professional could use a headline like "Results-driven Digital Marketer | SEO Specialist | Content Strategist." You attract the right audience once you ***use specific keywords*** that highlight your unique value proposition.

Profile Picture:

Your profile picture is the first visual representation of yourself that LinkedIn users see. Choose a high-quality, professional-looking photograph that aligns with your industry and conveys a sense of trust and approachability. Dress appropriately for your field, maintain good posture, and ensure your face is clearly visible. Remember, a genuine smile can go a long way in making a positive impression. Your profile picture should be professional and friendly. A high-quality image of you alone, with a plain or simple background, is ideal. Avoid using selfies or casual photos, which can give off an unprofessional vibe.

On LinkedIn, everything is about credibility and trust. Your personal brand is built on these two pillars. You also have the option of adding a LinkedIn profile video. Please note that you can only record or upload a profile video from the LinkedIn mobile app!

Banner Image:

The banner Image at the top of your LinkedIn profile lets you showcase your personality or professional branding. Select an image that reflects your industry, interests, or personal brand.

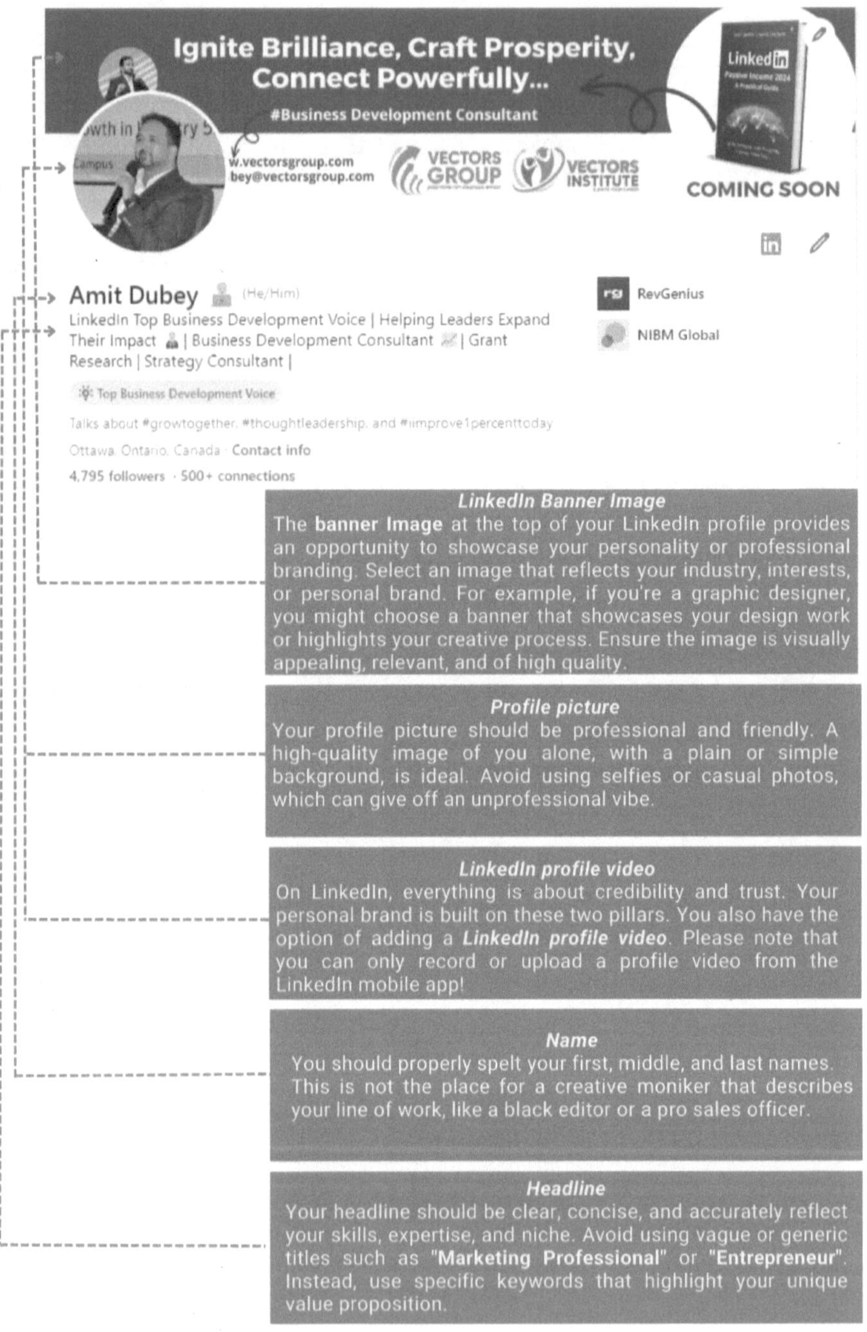

For example, if you're a graphic designer, you might choose a banner that showcases your design work or highlights your creative process. Ensure the image is visually appealing, relevant, and of high quality.

How do you optimize your headline, profile picture, and banner image?

To optimize your headline, profile picture, and banner image, follow these practical steps:

Headline Optimization:

a. *Identify relevant keywords:* Research the keywords commonly used in your industry or niche. Incorporate these keywords into your headline to improve your visibility in LinkedIn searches.

b. *Showcase your expertise:* Highlight your key skills, accomplishments, or areas of specialization likely to attract passive income opportunities.

c. *Be concise and impactful:* Craft a headline that succinctly captures your professional identity and value proposition, keeping it under 120 characters.

Profile Picture Optimization:

a. *Choose a professional-looking photo:* Dress professionally and ensure the photo represents your industry and desired professional image.

b. *Use a high-quality image:* Avoid blurry or low-resolution images that may convey unprofessionalism or lack of attention to detail.

c. *Keep it up to date:* Regularly update your profile picture to reflect your current appearance, ensuring it matches your professional persona.

Banner image Optimization:

a. *Align with your personal brand:* Select a banner image that reinforces your professional brand or conveys your expertise. It should be consistent with your industry and the message you want to convey.

b. *Maintain visual appeal:* Use high-quality images with vibrant colors and clear visuals to grab attention.

c. *Consider customization:* Leverage design tools to create a customized banner that stands out and represents your personal or professional brand effectively.

Remember, your headline, profile picture, and banner image are crucial in making a strong first impression on potential passive income opportunities. By optimizing these elements, you increase your chances of attracting the right opportunities and establishing yourself as a reliable and competent professional on LinkedIn.

Step 2: Craft a Compelling Summary

Why Craft a Compelling Summary?

Crafting a compelling summary for your LinkedIn profile is essential in attracting passive income opportunities. It is a powerful tool for engaging potential clients or customers and making lasting impressions. A well-crafted summary allows you to showcase your unique value proposition and communicate how you can solve their problems. By investing time and effort into creating an impactful summary, you increase your chances of capturing the attention of passive income prospects.

What to Consider When Crafting Your Summary?

When crafting your summary, consider the following elements to make it compelling:

- **Showcase your skills and experience:** Highlight your key skills, expertise, and relevant experience that position you as a valuable resource in your industry or niche. Focus on showcasing your achievements and the specific results you have achieved for clients or employers.
- **Communicate your unique value proposition:** Differentiate yourself from others in your industry by clearly articulating what sets you apart. Identify your unique strengths, passions, or approaches that make you an attractive option for passive income opportunities.
- **Address the needs of potential clients or customers:** Understand the pain points and challenges your target audience faces. Explain how your skills, knowledge, or products/services can help them overcome those challenges and achieve their goals.

How to Craft a Compelling Summary?

To craft a compelling summary that captures the attention of potential clients or customers, follow these steps:

- **Start with a captivating hook:** Begin your summary with an attention-grabbing statement or question that piques curiosity and compels readers to continue reading.
- **Tell your story:** Share your professional journey and experiences concisely yet engagingly. Focus on key milestones, turning points, or experiences that have shaped your expertise and credibility.
- **Highlight your achievements:** Showcase your notable accomplishments and the impact you have made in your field. Quantify your successes whenever possible to provide tangible evidence of your capabilities.
- **Demonstrate your expertise:** Explain your core competencies, areas of specialization, and the unique skills that make you stand out. Use specific examples or case studies to illustrate your expertise and show how you have delivered results for clients or employers.
- **Use a conversational tone:** Write in a friendly, approachable tone to connect with your readers personally. Avoid using jargon or technical terms that may alienate or confuse them.
- **Keep it concise and scannable:** Remember that LinkedIn users have limited attention spans. Keep your summary concise, using short paragraphs, bullet points, or subheadings to break up the text and make it easier to read and understand.
- **Call to action:** End your summary with a clear call to action, inviting readers to connect with you, explore your work further, or contact you for potential passive income opportunities.

Following these steps, you can create a compelling summary that effectively communicates your value proposition and entices potential clients or customers to engage with you. A well-crafted summary is persuasive in attracting passive income opportunities and establishing yourself as a trusted professional on LinkedIn.

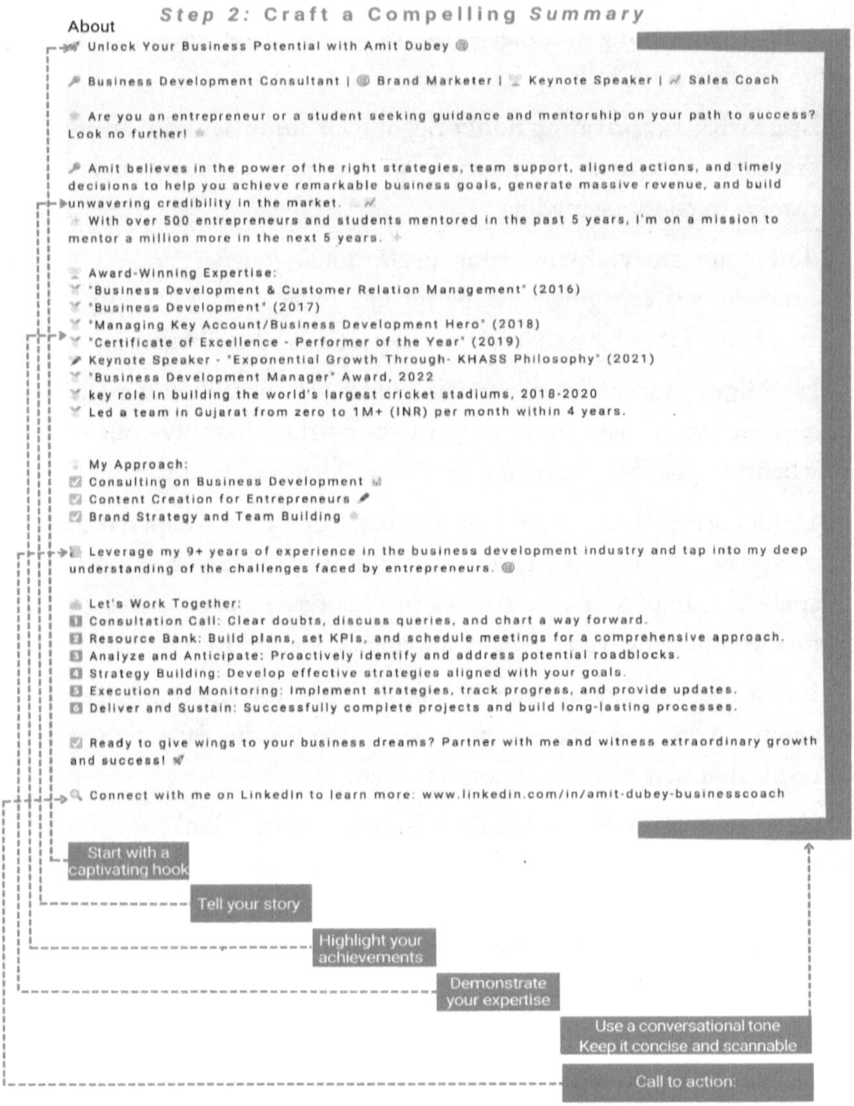

Step 2: Craft a Compelling Summary

About

Unlock Your Business Potential with Amit Dubey

Business Development Consultant | Brand Marketer | Keynote Speaker | Sales Coach

Are you an entrepreneur or a student seeking guidance and mentorship on your path to success? Look no further!

Amit believes in the power of the right strategies, team support, aligned actions, and timely decisions to help you achieve remarkable business goals, generate massive revenue, and build unwavering credibility in the market.

With over 500 entrepreneurs and students mentored in the past 5 years, I'm on a mission to mentor a million more in the next 5 years.

Award-Winning Expertise:
"Business Development & Customer Relation Management" (2016)
"Business Development" (2017)
"Managing Key Account/Business Development Hero" (2018)
"Certificate of Excellence - Performer of the Year" (2019)
Keynote Speaker - "Exponential Growth Through- KHASS Philosophy" (2021)
"Business Development Manager" Award, 2022
key role in building the world's largest cricket stadiums, 2018-2020
Led a team in Gujarat from zero to 1M+ (INR) per month within 4 years.

My Approach:
Consulting on Business Development
Content Creation for Entrepreneurs
Brand Strategy and Team Building

Leverage my 9+ years of experience in the business development industry and tap into my deep understanding of the challenges faced by entrepreneurs.

Let's Work Together:
1 Consultation Call: Clear doubts, discuss queries, and chart a way forward.
2 Resource Bank: Build plans, set KPIs, and schedule meetings for a comprehensive approach.
3 Analyze and Anticipate: Proactively identify and address potential roadblocks.
4 Strategy Building: Develop effective strategies aligned with your goals.
5 Execution and Monitoring: Implement strategies, track progress, and provide updates.
6 Deliver and Sustain: Successfully complete projects and build long-lasting processes.

Ready to give wings to your business dreams? Partner with me and witness extraordinary growth and success!

Connect with me on LinkedIn to learn more: www.linkedin.com/in/amit-dubey-businesscoach

Start with a captivating hook

Tell your story

Highlight your achievements

Demonstrate your expertise

Use a conversational tone
Keep it concise and scannable

Call to action:

Step 3: Highlight Your Experience and Top Skills (New Feature)

Why Highlight Your Experience and Top Skills?

Highlighting your experience and top skills on your LinkedIn profile is crucial for attracting passive income opportunities. This section showcases your professional journey, demonstrating your expertise, accomplishments, and the value you can bring to potential clients or customers. By effectively highlighting your experience and top skills, you establish yourself as a competent and credible professional, increasing your chances of securing passive income ventures. Your experience section is the heart of your LinkedIn profile. This is also an excellent place to showcase any awards or accolades you've received and any certifications or credentials you hold.

When describing your work experience, focus on the impact you've made in your role. **For example, instead of saying, "Managed a team of 5 people", say, "Led a team of 5 people, resulting in a 30% increase in productivity".** This shows potential clients or customers that you're results-driven and can provide value.

When strategically optimizing your LinkedIn profile to amplify your passive income prospects, meticulous consideration of key elements becomes imperative. Before embarking on any modifications, it's essential to define precisely the passive income sources you're targeting. This clarity serves as the compass guiding each adjustment to ensure alignment with your ultimate financial goals.

1. Relevance to Passive Income Goals:Tailoring your experience and highlighting your skills should be a purposeful exercise. Direct these aspects to seamlessly align with the needs and preferences of your intended audience for passive income. Emphasize facets of your professional background that directly resonate with the industry, niche, or specific projects integral to your passive income endeavors.

2. Demonstrating Impact and Results:Elevate your profile by transcending the conventional approach of merely listing job responsibilities. Instead, focus on articulating the tangible outcomes and achievements attained in each professional role. Whether it's contributing to revenue growth, achieving cost savings, orchestrating process improvements, or successfully completing pivotal projects, emphasize results that distinctly contribute to and support your targeted passive income goals.

3. Showcasing Awards and Certifications: In the pursuit of building credibility, draw attention to any awards, accolades, or industry certifications you've garnered. These accolades serve as compelling validations of your expertise and proficiency. When strategically positioned, they significantly enhance your professional standing, reinforcing your credibility specifically within the context of your chosen passive income sources.

   In essence, every modification in your profile should be a deliberate step towards fortifying your position in the landscape of passive income on LinkedIn. By ensuring that each change is intricately tied to your targeted income streams, you set the stage for a profile that not only reflects your professional journey but also positions you strategically for the passive income success you aspire to achieve.

How do you highlight your experience and top skills?

To effectively highlight your experience and top skills on your LinkedIn profile, follow these steps:

- **Organize your experience section:** Present your work experience in reverse chronological order, starting with your current or most recent position. Include the company name, job title, employment dates, and a concise description of your role.
- **Utilize bullet points:** Use bullet points to highlight your key accomplishments and responsibilities in each position. Focus on quantifiable achievements, specific projects you've worked on, and any notable contributions you've made.
- **Showcase the impact:** Emphasize the results and impact of your work by highlighting key achievements. Use metrics, percentages, or concrete examples to demonstrate how your efforts have benefited the company or clients you have served.
- **Incorporate relevant keywords:** Sprinkle relevant keywords throughout your experience section to optimize your profile for LinkedIn's search algorithm. This increases your visibility to potential passive income prospects searching for professionals with specific skills or expertise.

- **Highlight top skills:** Use LinkedIn's "Featured Skills & Endorsements" section to showcase your top skills. Select the most relevant skills for your target audience and those with the highest endorsements. This emphasizes your areas of expertise and helps potential clients or customers understand your capabilities.
- **Leverage multimedia and recommendations:** Enhance your experience section by incorporating multimedia elements such as links to relevant projects, articles, or presentations. Additionally, request recommendations from colleagues, clients, or supervisors to provide social proof of your skills and capabilities.

Following these steps, you can effectively highlight your experience and top skills, demonstrating your value and expertise to potential passive income opportunities. A well-crafted experience section increases your credibility and positions you as a qualified professional worth considering for lucrative ventures.

Step 4: Showcase Your Skills

The skills section of your profile allows you to highlight your specific areas of expertise. List skills relevant to the niche you're targeting for passive income opportunities, and prioritize the skills most important for your ideal clients or customers.

LinkedIn allows you to list up to ***50 skills*** on your profile. Choose skills you have experience in and can confidently speak to if asked. Also, make sure to keep your skills up to date and remove any skills that are no longer relevant.

Business Development Consultant (Intrapreneur)
Vectors Group · Full-time
Sep 2022 - Present · 10 mos
Ottawa, Ontario, Canada
helped me get this job
Skills: Time Management · Business Strategy · Training & Development · Business Development · Sales
Sign Up | LinkedIn
A conversation for training & development in the nonprofit organization.
Business Development Manager (Intrapreneur)
Uniquo
Jan 2015 - Aug 2022 · 7 yrs 8 mos
Mulund, Maharashtra, India
BUSINESS DEVELOPMENT MANAGER (Intrapreneur) @ UNIQUO Group
1st UNIQUO
In my role, I am responsible for the operation and entire marketing & sales process from cold calling; to order confirmation to smooth operation. I am a key accountable person of the Gujarat, UP, Bihar, and Delhi team dealing with inspection & certification, the auditing process, and, supporting my colleagues and customer. I am involved with multiple activities from cross-checking invoices to the work order, in addition, I manage and collocate customer databases and act as a primary responder for the phone call. I am responsible for the inspection of machinery.
PROGRAM COORDINATOR @ ICLM
2nd INSTITUTE OF CONSTRUCTION EQUIPMENTS & LIFTING MACHINES
Recognized by: Director of industrial safety and Health, Gujarat (D.I.S.H)
This role required that I undertake general day-to-day training and organized tasks and duties including sales & marketing, meeting and greeting customers, answering calls and dealing with requirements, and, organizing in-house and off-site training & certification. It includes a meeting with the government directors and officers. Collaboration with an international body for the training and certification session. I am also accountable for preparing the public workshops calendar. I also conducted a vocational training session on the behalf of our institute. I am a keynote speaker who talks about personal development and career growth.
Skills: New Business Development · Business Planning · Business Process Improvement · Business Relationship Management · Business Management · International Business · Strategic Planning · Business-to-Business (B2B) · Business Strategy · Training · Negotiation · Training & Development · Training Delivery · Business Development · Sales

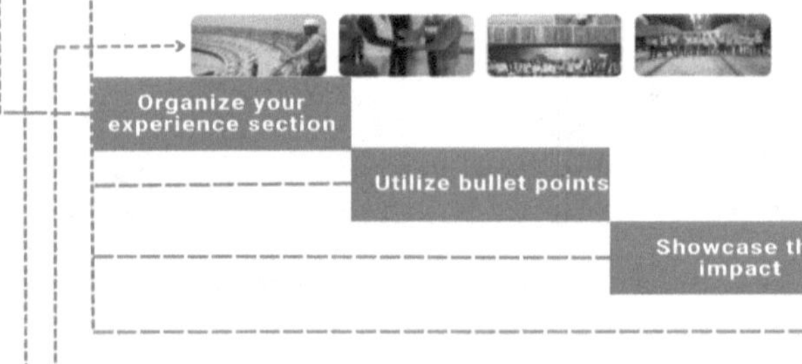
Organize your experience section
Utilize bullet points
Showcase the impact
Incorporate relevant keywords
Highlight top skills
Leverage multimedia and recommendations

Step 5: Build Your Network

Why Build Your Network?

Building a strong network on LinkedIn is crucial for attracting passive income opportunities. Your network is a valuable resource for potential collaborations, referrals, and industry insights. Connecting with relevant professionals expands your reach and increases the chances of discovering lucrative passive income prospects. Building a network allows you to tap into the power of relationships and leverage collective knowledge. Start by connecting with people you already know, such as colleagues, former classmates, or industry peers. Then, expand your network by connecting with people in your target niche or industry. Remember to personalize your connection requests and always send a message thanking people for accepting your request.

It's important to note that building a strong network isn't about the quantity of connections but the quality. ***Focus on building relationships*** with people in your network by engaging with their content and sharing your own.

What to Consider When Engaging With Your Network?

When delving into interactions within your LinkedIn network with the aim of fostering meaningful connections and unlocking passive income opportunities, meticulous consideration of the following factors is paramount:

1. Alignment with Passive Income Goals: Tailor your engagements to align with the type of passive income you seek. Whether it's through affiliations, partnerships, or knowledge-sharing, ensure your interactions resonate with the specific passive income streams you're targeting.
2. Strategic Value-Driven Contributions: Elevate your engagement strategy by focusing on value-driven contributions. Tailor your content and comments to be insightful, relevant, and directly linked to your passive income objectives. Offer solutions, share expertise, and strategically position yourself as a valuable asset within your network.

3. Customization for Targeted Connections:Consider the profiles and preferences of your connections. Personalize your interactions to match the professional journeys and interests of specific individuals within your network who align with your passive income goals. A nuanced approach demonstrates a tailored commitment to each connection's success.
4. Strategic Consistency and Regular Engagement: Maintain a consistent presence on LinkedIn strategically. Regularly engaging with your network's content not only keeps you visible but also reinforces your commitment to the community. Dedicate specific time slots to engage, respond thoughtfully to comments, and actively participate in discussions that align with your passive income pursuits.
5. Strategic Personalized Messages and Check-ins: Elevate your connection-building efforts by sending personalized messages strategically. Use these messages to check in on your connections' professional journeys, extend congratulations on achievements, and share resources tailored to their interests. Strategic personalization reinforces the authenticity of your connection-building efforts.
6. Strategic Participation in LinkedIn Groups: Engage strategically in LinkedIn groups that align with your passive income goals. Share your expertise, answer questions thoughtfully, and participate in discussions relevant to your niche. This strategic involvement expands your network within a targeted context, establishing you as a niche authority and attracting potential passive income opportunities in a deliberate manner.

How to Build Your Network?

To effectively build your network on LinkedIn and attract passive income opportunities, follow these steps:

- **Connect with people you know:** Connect with colleagues, former classmates, friends, and acquaintances. These connections form the foundation of your network and can introduce you to new opportunities or refer you to potential clients or customers.
- **Expand your network strategically:** Research and identify professionals in your target niche or industry who align with your passive income goals. Send personalized connection requests, explaining why you find their

work relevant or interesting. Look for mutual connections or common interests to establish a stronger connection.

- **Engage with your connections:** Regularly engage with the content of your connections by liking, commenting on, and sharing their posts. This interaction strengthens your relationship and increases your visibility within their networks.
- **Participate in LinkedIn groups:** Join relevant LinkedIn groups and actively participate in discussions. Contribute valuable insights, ask thoughtful questions, and connect with like-minded professionals who share your interests or goals.
- **Attend industry events and webinars:** Take advantage of virtual or in-person industry events, conferences, and webinars. These platforms provide excellent opportunities to network with professionals in your field and expand your connections.
- **Follow up and express gratitude:** Whenever someone accepts your connection request or engages with your content, take the time to send a personalized message expressing your gratitude. Building and maintaining relationships is key to unlocking passive income opportunities.

By following these steps, you can build a valuable network on LinkedIn that increases your visibility, fosters collaborations, and attracts passive income opportunities. Remember to be genuine, professional, and proactive in nurturing and expanding your network.

Step 6: Engage With Your Network

Why Engage With Your Network?

Engaging with your network on LinkedIn is crucial for building relationships, fostering connections, and establishing yourself as an authority in your niche. By actively participating in conversations, commenting on posts, sharing valuable content, and reaching out to individuals personally, you demonstrate your interest, expertise, and commitment to building meaningful connections. Engaging with your network helps you stay top of mind and build trust with potential clients or customers, increasing the likelihood of attracting passive income opportunities.

What to Consider When Engaging With Your Network?

When engaging with your network on LinkedIn, consider the following factors to make your interactions effective and meaningful:

- **Authenticity and genuine interest:** Approach your interactions with authenticity and a genuine interest in the conversations and content your connections share. Be thoughtful and respectful in your comments and messages, showing that you value their perspectives and contributions.
- **Value-driven contributions:** Share insightful and relevant content to your network. Offer thoughtful comments that contribute to the conversation and demonstrate your expertise. Focus on sharing knowledge, providing solutions, and supporting others in your network.
- **Consistency and regular engagement:** Maintain a consistent presence on LinkedIn by regularly engaging with your network's content. Consistency helps you stay visible and fosters stronger connections. Aim to allocate dedicated time for engaging on the platform, responding to comments, and actively participating in discussions.
- **Personalized messages and check-ins:** Take the time to send personalized messages to your connections to check in on their professional journey, congratulate them on their achievements, or share relevant resources. Personalized messages show you value the relationship and are invested in their success.
- **Active participation in LinkedIn groups:** Engage actively in relevant LinkedIn groups by sharing your expertise, answering questions, and participating in discussions. This helps you expand your network, establish yourself as an authority in your niche, and attract potential passive income opportunities.

How to Engage With Your Network?

To effectively engage with your network on LinkedIn and maximize your chances of attracting passive income opportunities, follow these steps:

- **Comment on posts:** Regularly comment on the posts shared by your connections. Offer insightful perspectives, ask thoughtful questions, or share relevant experiences related to the content. Engaging in meaningful conversations helps build rapport and visibility within your network.

- **Share valuable content:** Share articles, industry news, or helpful resources that align with your expertise and can benefit your connections. Focus on providing value and insights that resonate with your target audience.
- **Support and promote your connections:** Share the content of your connections with your network, giving credit to the original creators. This helps them increase their visibility, strengthens your relationship, and encourages reciprocal support.
- **Send personalized messages:** Reach out to your connections with personalized messages, checking in on their professional journey or sharing relevant insights or opportunities. Personalized messages show that you value the relationship and are genuinely interested in their success.
- **Engage in LinkedIn groups:** Participate actively in relevant LinkedIn groups by sharing your expertise, engaging in discussions, and providing valuable insights. This helps you expand your network, connect with industry peers, and establish yourself as an authority in your niche.
- **Respond to comments and messages:** Take the time to respond to comments on your posts or messages you receive. Prompt and thoughtful responses show your professionalism and dedication to building relationships.

By following these steps, you can actively engage with your network on LinkedIn, establish your authority, and build meaningful relationships. Regular and genuine engagement enhances visibility, increases trust, and attracts potential passive income opportunities.

Step 7: Keep Your Profile Up to Date

Why Keep Your Profile Up to Date?

It's essential to keep your LinkedIn profile up to date. Keeping your LinkedIn profile updated is crucial for attracting passive income opportunities. An updated profile demonstrates your professionalism, commitment to personal branding, and active engagement on the platform. Regularly updating your profile with new skills, experiences, and accomplishments ensures that potential clients or customers see the most accurate and relevant representation of your expertise. Additionally, an up-to-date profile increases your visibility in LinkedIn searches and signals that you are serious about your professional presence. It's also a good idea to regularly review your profile and make updates as needed to ensure it's always optimized for your niche.

What to Consider When Keeping Your Profile Up to Date?

When maintaining an up-to-date LinkedIn profile, consider the following factors to ensure its effectiveness:

- **Current and relevant information:** Regularly review and update your profile with the latest information regarding your skills, experiences, achievements, and qualifications. Include recent projects, certifications, promotions, or accomplishments showcasing your growth and expertise.
- **Consistent branding:** Ensure your profile aligns with your personal brand and the niche or industry you want to attract passive income opportunities. Use consistent messaging, visual elements, and keywords to create a cohesive and professional impression.
- **Optimize for your niche:** Regularly review your profile to ensure it is optimized for your target niche. Incorporate industry-specific keywords and emphasize the skills, experiences, or accomplishments that are most relevant to attracting passive income opportunities within your desired field.
- **Showcase ongoing professional development:** Highlight any ongoing professional development initiatives, such as courses, workshops, or conferences you have attended. This demonstrates your commitment to staying updated with industry trends and continuously improving your skills.
- **Request and display recommendations:** Regularly request recommendations from colleagues, clients, or supervisors who can vouch for your skills and work ethic. Displaying these recommendations on your profile adds credibility and builds trust with potential clients or customers.

How do you keep your profile up to date?

To keep your LinkedIn profile up to date and maximize its impact in attracting passive income opportunities, follow these steps:

- **Regularly review your profile:** Set aside time periodically to review your profile and assess if any information needs updating. Check for outdated job titles, descriptions, or contact details and make the necessary updates.
- **Add new skills and experiences:** As you acquire new skills, complete projects, or gain relevant experiences, promptly add them to your profile. Highlight the value and impact you have made in your roles to showcase your expertise.
- **Update your headline and summary:** Keep your headline and summary section current and engaging. Use compelling language to describe your unique value proposition and how you can help potential clients or customers. Tailor these sections to reflect your latest achievements and goals.
- **Incorporate media and visual elements:** Utilize LinkedIn's media features to showcase your work, such as project samples, presentations, or articles. Update your profile and banner photos to reflect your professional image and branding.
- **Stay active and engage:** Regularly engage with your network, share valuable content, and participate in relevant discussions. Being active on the platform helps you stay connected, increase visibility, and attract potential passive income opportunities.
- **Seek feedback and iterate:** Request feedback from trusted connections or mentors to get insights into areas where you can further improve your profile. Act on the feedback received and iterated on your profile to ensure it consistently aligns with your goals and attracts the right audience.

By following these steps and keeping your LinkedIn profile current, you ensure that potential clients or customers see an accurate and compelling representation of your skills and expertise. An up-to-date profile enhances your professional image, increases visibility, and maximizes your chances of attracting passive income opportunities.

Step 8: Unleashing the Power of LinkedIn's Feature Section

LinkedIn has established itself as the premier professional networking platform in today's digital age, connecting millions of professionals, companies, and job seekers worldwide. With its ever-evolving suite of features, LinkedIn continues to empower individuals and businesses to build their professional brands, expand their networks, and discover new opportunities.

Why Unleashing the Power of LinkedIn's Feature Section?

LinkedIn's Feature Section is a dynamic platform element designed to help professionals showcase their expertise, achievements, and interests. It serves as a strategic tool to shape and enhance one's personal brand, enabling users to convey a compelling narrative about their professional journey and strengths. The Feature Section allows individuals to stand out in a competitive market, attract the attention of potential employers, clients, or collaborators, and establish credibility and trust within their network.

What to Consider when Maximizing the Feature Section's Impact?

LinkedIn's Feature Section presents countless opportunities to unlock professional growth and success when effectively utilized. Here are some key benefits:

- **Enhanced visibility and credibility:** A well-curated Feature Section can significantly improve your professional visibility, making you stand out from the crowd. You can establish credibility, instill trust, and attract relevant opportunities by showcasing your expertise and achievements.
- **Increased engagement and networking:** The Feature Section acts as a conversation starter, facilitating meaningful interactions with your network. Visitors can engage with your content, leave comments, and start conversations, enabling you to expand your professional connections and build valuable relationships.
- **Personalized branding:** By leveraging the Feature Section, you can sculpt a personalized brand narrative that aligns with your professional goals and values. It allows you to shape how others perceive you and helps you differentiate yourself from competitors.

- **Career advancement opportunities:** An impactful Feature Section can catch the attention of recruiters, hiring managers, and potential clients, leading to exciting career advancement opportunities. It positions you as a standout candidate or an attractive service provider, increasing your chances of securing desirable roles or projects.

How: Utilizing the Feature Section Effectively

To harness the power of the Feature Section, professionals must strategically curate and present their content to align with their career goals. Here are some essential tips to consider:

- **Define your objective:** Determine the primary purpose of your Feature Section. Are you aiming to highlight your expertise, showcase your portfolio, or demonstrate thought leadership? Clarifying your objective will guide your content selection and presentation approach.
- **Craft a captivating headline:** Grab visitors' attention with a concise and compelling headline that communicates your professional value proposition. Tailor it to resonate with your target audience and emphasize your unique strengths.
- **Leverage media elements:** The Feature Section allows you to incorporate various media, such as articles, posts, documents, images, and videos. Capitalize on this opportunity by showcasing your best work, multimedia presentations, testimonials, or relevant industry publications to reinforce your expertise.
- **Share success stories:** Highlight your accomplishments, projects, and success stories to effectively demonstrate your skills and capabilities. Use this section to showcase measurable results, testimonials, or case studies illustrating your impact and value.
- **Curate thought leadership content:** Establish yourself as an industry authority by sharing thought-provoking insights, trends, and expert opinions. Publish articles or links to external content that showcases your expertise and demonstrates your commitment to staying abreast of industry developments.
- **Update regularly:** Keep your Feature Section up to date with fresh content. Regularly refresh your portfolio, articles, or media to reflect

your most recent achievements and ensure visitors perceive you as an active and engaged professional.

Feature Section is crucial in building a compelling professional brand and accelerating career growth. By adopting a strategic approach, curating engaging content, and staying true to your professional narrative, you can leverage this platform element to establish credibility, expand your network, and seize exciting opportunities. Remember, the Feature Section is your canvas to showcase your expertise, so make the most of it and let your professional story shine.

Regenerate response

Following these steps, you can build a strong LinkedIn profile to attract potential passive income opportunities. Remember to focus on what makes you unique and showcase your skills and expertise clearly and compellingly.

Here's a checklist summarizing the steps to building a strong LinkedIn profile to attract passive income opportunities:

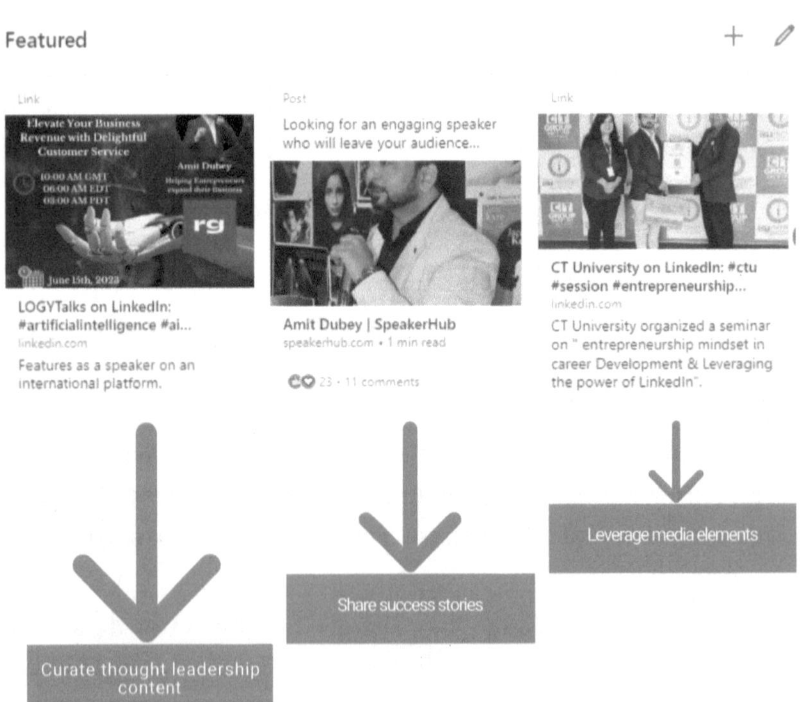

Step 9: Customize your LinkedIn URL.

Customizing your LinkedIn URL is a simple yet impactful way to enhance your personal brand and make your profile more professional and easily shareable. By default, LinkedIn assigns a unique URL to each user's profile, typically consisting of random numbers and letters. However, LinkedIn allows users to customize their URLs to reflect their name or professional identity. Here's how you can customize your LinkedIn URL:

- Sign into your LinkedIn account: Visit the LinkedIn website and sign in using your credentials.
- Access your profile: Click on "Me" in the top navigation bar to access your profile.
- Edit your public profile settings: On your profile page, click on the "Edit public profile & URL" option on the right-hand side of the screen. It may be under your profile photo or the "More" dropdown menu.
- Customize your URL: On the right-hand side of the page, you will see the "Edit URL" section. Here, you can see your current LinkedIn URL and an option to edit it. Click on the pencil icon next to your URL.
- Choose your custom URL: In the editing field, enter your desired custom URL in the editing field. It's recommended to use your full name or a professional variation of your name. Avoid using spaces, special characters, or excessive symbols to ensure simplicity and ease of use.
- Verify availability and save changes: LinkedIn will automatically check the availability of your chosen custom URL. If it's available, a green checkmark will appear. If it's not available, you'll need to try different variations until you find an available option. Once you find an available custom URL, click on "Save" to confirm your changes.

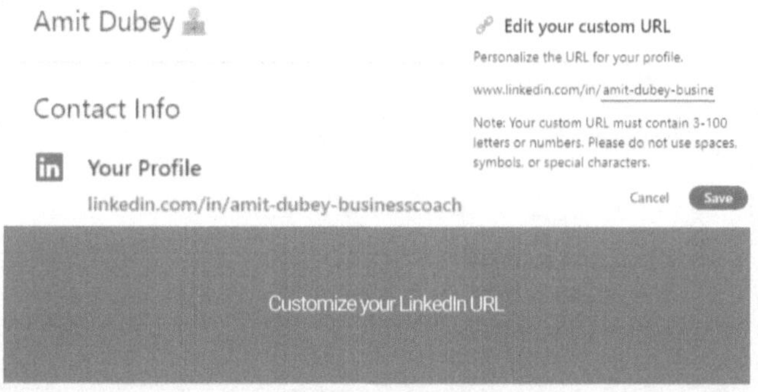

- Test your new URL: After saving your custom URL, test it by typing it into a web browser to ensure it directs to your LinkedIn profile. Also, update any online profiles, resumes, or business cards with your new custom URL to maintain consistency across your professional presence.

Remember that once you've customized your LinkedIn URL, it becomes a permanent link associated with your profile. Therefore, choose a URL that represents your professional identity and is easy for others to remember and access.

- Optimize your headline and profile picture, and consider adding a profile video to enhance credibility
- Craft a compelling summary that showcases your unique value proposition
- Highlight your relevant experience and accomplishments, using bullet points to highlight your key achievements
- Showcase your skills, prioritizing those that are most relevant to your target niche or industry
- Build a strong network by connecting with people you know and those in your target niche or industry
- Engage with your network by commenting on posts, sharing content, and sending personalized messages
- Keep your profile updated by adding new skills, experiences, or accomplishments and regularly reviewing it for optimization.

By completing these steps, you'll have a strong LinkedIn profile that positions you as an authority in your niche and attracts potential passive income opportunities.

Next Chapter: Identifying and Targeting Profitable LinkedIn Niches in 2024

Chapter 3

Identifying and Targeting Profitable LinkedIn Niches in 2024

"Want passive income on LinkedIn? Start by choosing your niche right. Let's explore steps for your success."

Step 1: Research Your Interests, Skills, and Market Demand or Problem Statement.

Meet Naina-The Writer, a marketing enthusiast with a knack for content creation. As she delves into identifying a niche, she reflects on her passions and skills. What is she truly good at? Where does her heart lie? Recognizing the market demand, she identifies a problem statement: small businesses struggling with content marketing on LinkedIn.

Step 2: Identify Market Gaps

Naina knows she's onto something, but where's the gap? It's not just about content marketing; it's about finding a niche within. She researches and discovers that while many offer general content services, there's a lack of specialized LinkedIn content strategies. The gap is evident – small businesses need tailored content for LinkedIn success.

Example: Consider a small tech startup. They have a great product but lack engaging LinkedIn content.Naina's niche is to fill this gap by providing targeted content that resonates with the tech industry's audience.

Step 3: Research Your Competition

Naina scouts her competition – other content creators on LinkedIn. She analyzes their profiles, scrutinizes their offerings, and identifies a void. Most focus on broad social media content, missing the specificity of LinkedIn. This is her chance to stand out.

Example: A competitor might offer generic social media content services. Naina aims to differentiate by honing in on the LinkedIn platform, showcasing her expertise in crafting content that speaks directly to LinkedIn's audience.

Step 4: Define Your Unique Value Proposition

Now, Naina defines her unique value proposition. What sets her apart? It's not just about content creation; it's about LinkedIn-centric content that drives engagement. Her proposition: "Elevate Your Brand on LinkedIn with Tailored Content Strategies." This becomes the anchor for her LinkedIn profile.

Example: Naina's unique value proposition positions her as the LinkedIn content specialist, promising clients a strategic approach that goes beyond generic social media content.

Step 5: Identify Your Target Audience

With a clear proposition, Naina identifies her target audience. Small tech businesses struggling to make an impact on LinkedIn become her focus. She delves into their pain points, understanding their need for specialized content that resonates with their industry.

Example: A tech startup in need of LinkedIn content might face challenges in standing out in a crowded market. Naina aims to tailor her services to address these specific challenges.

Step 6: Test Your Niche

Time to test the waters. Naina reaches out to potential clients offering a free LinkedIn content consultation. This step is crucial – it's about validating her niche. Are businesses interested in specialized LinkedIn content? The feedback from consultations will shape her next move.

Example: Naina offers free LinkedIn content consultations to a few tech startups. Their response and interest will indicate if there's a real demand for her niche service.

Step 7: Refine Your Approach

The feedback is in, and now Naina refines her approach. Perhaps she discovers that while lead generation content is essential, these startups are also struggling with profile optimization. She adjusts her services and messaging accordingly.

Example: Based on feedback, Naina realizes that tech startups not only need content but also guidance on optimizing their LinkedIn profiles for visibility. She refines her approach to offer a comprehensive LinkedIn brand strategy.

In this chapter, we embarked on the journey of uncovering profitable LinkedIn niches, understanding that success in passive income hinges on strategic niche selection. We followed the story of Naina, a marketing enthusiast, as she navigated the steps to identify a niche that not only aligned with her skills and passions but also addressed a market gap.

Here's a quick recap of the key steps:

1 Research Your Interests, Skills, and Market Demand:

- Identify your passions and expertise.
- Recognize a problem statement or market demand.

2. Identify Market Gaps:
    - Search for areas within your expertise with high demand but low supply.
    - Look for underserved niches or industries.
3. Research Your Competition:
    - Analyze competitors within your potential niche.
    - Identify opportunities to differentiate yourself.
4. Define Your Unique Value Proposition (UVP):
    - Clearly articulate what sets you apart.
    - Develop a compelling UVP that highlights your specialized offering.
5. Identify Your Target Audience:
    - Define your ideal client or customer within your chosen niche.
    - Understand their pain points and needs.
6. Test Your Niche:
    - Reach out to potential clients for feedback.
    - Offer a trial or consultation to gauge interest and demand.
7. Refine Your Approach Based on Feedback:
    - Use feedback to adjust your services, messaging, or target audience.
    - Pivot or expand your offerings as needed.

Next Chapter: Creating Content that Drives Passive Income on LinkedIn in 2024

Chapter 4

Creating Content that Drives Passive Income on LinkedIn in 2024

"In the world of LinkedIn, your content is your currency. Craft it wisely, and watch the passive income flow in." Amit Dubey

In the vast and dynamic realm of LinkedIn, your content is your currency, and understanding its potential is the key to unlocking the doors of passive income. This chapter aims to delve into the art of content creation, addressing the most crucial questions that arise in the world of LinkedIn.

The Silent Majority: Unleashing the Power of Creation

LinkedIn boasts an impressive 1 billion members spread across more than 200 countries and territories. However, the disparity between potential and reality is striking—only a million users have ventured into publishing articles, and a mere 3 million share content weekly. This glaring gap highlights an immense opportunity for those willing to step into the content creation arena.

The Silence of the Audiences: The Underutilized Potential

LinkedIn's audience is largely silent, with a staggering 90% passively observing the platform, 6-8% engaging with content, and a mere 1-2% actively creating.

This silent majority represents an untapped well of potential for those ready to fill the void.

Analyzing the Echo of Engagement: The Follower Paradox

In a personal exploration of 20 posts, totaling over 15k engagements, a profound revelation surfaced. A mere 20% of engagement emanated from connections and followers, while the remaining 80% surged from unknown corners. This data underscores a critical point: the quality of your content eclipses the sheer quantity of followers.

Crafting Content - The Duo: Participation Matters

The journey of content creation on LinkedIn splits into two dimensions: crafting content for your profile and contributing to others' profiles. Beyond broadcasting your own narrative, active engagement with the content of your target audience sparks a reciprocity that amplifies your reach and influence.

Cracking the Virality Conundrum: The Role of Consistency

The quest for viral content is a labyrinth without a map. There's no magic formula, and expectations rarely align with reality. However, amidst this uncertainty, one constant shines through—consistency. Regular, meaningful contributions become the unyielding growth hack.

The Tapestry of LinkedIn Content: Crafting for Impact

What Content to Create:

1 Storytelling Takes Center Stage:
    - Develop narratives that resonate, connecting on a personal and emotional level.
    - Share experiences, anecdotes, and lessons learned, fostering a relatable connection with your audience.

2 Trend Jacking with a Unique Perspective:

- Trend jacking isn't about copy-pasting; it's about infusing trends with your distinctive viewpoint.
- Add personal insights, reflections, or even a touch of humor to make your content stand out.

3 Voicing Opinions:

- Contribute to industry discussions by sharing your informed opinions.
- Develop a unique voice that adds value to conversations and positions you as a thought leader.

4 Delving into Case Studies:

- Share real-world examples and experiences.
- Extract lessons from case studies, providing valuable insights to your audience.

How to Create Content

1 Written Posts or LinkedIn Articles:

- Craft thought-provoking written content directly landing in your follower's email.
- Share comprehensive insights, analysis, and expert opinions.

2 Images: The Challenging Yet Pivotal Medium:

- Focus on precision when utilizing images.
- Choose visuals that amplify your message and resonate with your audience.

3 Video: The Face Value Medium:

- Engage authentically through video content.
- Leverage the power of storytelling, visuals, and personal connection.

4 Carousel/PDF: Early Adopter's Playground:

- Appeal to the early adopters by experimenting with carousel or PDF formats.
- Share detailed content, guides, or presentations in a format that stands out.

5 Audio Events: Discussing Hot Topics:
   - Engage in discussions on hot topics within your industry.
   - Collaborate with experts to add depth and varied perspectives.

6 Video Podcasts: Launching Products and Industry Discussions:
   - Use video podcasts as a platform to launch products.
   - Dive into industry-relevant discussions, providing valuable insights and fostering engagement.

The Crux: The Inconsistency in the Consistency

In the unpredictable tapestry of LinkedIn content, the constant is inconsistency. There's no foolproof guide, no guaranteed formula for virality. The art lies in adaptation, in the willingness to experiment. As you navigate this chapter, remember, your content on LinkedIn is not just a creation; it's a conversation, a gateway to a world where passive income flows in tandem with the captivating tales you unfold. So, let's dive in, craft, and captivate.

Chapter Summary: Crafting Content for LinkedIn Passive Income

This chapter unveiled the pivotal role of content on LinkedIn as the gateway to passive income. From exploring the silent majority in LinkedIn's vast audience to decoding the paradox of engagement, it emphasized the quality of content over follower count. The duo of crafting content for your profile and actively engaging with others' content emerged as a winning strategy. The journey of cracking the virality conundrum highlighted the consistency factor. The chapter also delved into the diverse tapestry of LinkedIn content, from Storiestelling to Trend Jacking and Voicing Opinions. The varied formats, from written posts to video podcasts, were explored, emphasizing the importance of adaptation and experimentation.

Implementation Checklist: Crafting LinkedIn Content for Impact

1 Define Your Niche and Audience:
- Identify the audience you want to engage.
- Define your niche to tailor content that resonates.

2 Craft Stories and Personal Narratives:
- Develop narratives that connect emotionally.
- Share personal experiences and anecdotes.

3 Trend Jacking with a Twist:
- Add a unique perspective to trending topics.
- Infuse trends with your distinctive viewpoint.

4 Voice Your Opinions:
- Contribute thoughtfully to industry discussions.
- Develop a unique voice that adds value.

5 Delve into Case Studies:
- Share real-world examples and lessons.
- Extract insights from case studies.

6 Experiment with Content Formats:
- Try written posts, images, videos, and more.
- Adapt content formats to your audience's preferences.

7 Engage Actively with Your Audience:
- Participate in discussions on others' content.
- Foster reciprocity for increased reach.

8 Consistency is Key:
- Regularly contribute meaningful content.
- Be consistent in engagement and posting.

9 Utilize Varied Content Formats:
- Experiment with written posts, images, videos, and podcasts.
- Tailor content formats to your message and audience.

10 Adapt and Experiment:
   - Be open to adapting your content strategy.
   - Experiment with different topics, formats, and styles.

Quick Hack: The 30:20 Rule for LinkedIn Engagement

Boost your LinkedIn post's visibility and interaction with the 30:20 rule:

1 Pre-Posting Engagement (30 Minutes Before):
   - Engage with other posts, LinkedIn News, or groups.
   - Write genuine comments on relevant content.
   - Use heart emojis instead of just liking posts.

2 Post-Posting Engagement (20 Minutes After):
   - Stay active and responsive for the next 20 minutes.
   - Reply promptly to comments on your post.
   - Foster communication by engaging with those who interact with your content.

This rule maximizes visibility, encourages meaningful interactions, and enhances the overall impact of your LinkedIn posts.

Next Chapter: Amplifying Influence – The Roadmap to a Thriving LinkedIn Following for Passive Income

Chapter 5

Amplifying Influence – The Roadmap to a Thriving LinkedIn Following for Passive Income

"Your first 4000 connections matter; they could be 4000 new opportunities in your success, so connect wisely." - Amit Dubey

Building a large and engaged LinkedIn following is critical for generating maximum passive income from the platform. In this chapter, we'll explore some effective strategies for growing your LinkedIn following and increasing engagement with your content.

- Optimize your LinkedIn profile: Your LinkedIn profile is often the first impression people have of you on the platform. Ensure your profile is complete, professional, and optimized for your niche. Use a high-quality profile picture, include a clear headline, and write a compelling summary that showcases your expertise and value proposition. Be sure to include relevant keywords to help people find you when searching for premia content in your niche.
- Consistently share high-quality content: Consistently sharing high-quality content is one of the most effective ways to attract followers and build engagement on LinkedIn. Ensure your content is relevant, informative, and valuable to your target audience. Use a mix of formats, such as text posts, images, videos, and articles, to keep your content

fresh and engaging. Use data and statistics to back up your claims, and include actionable tips and insights that your audience can apply to their own lives or businesses.

- Engage with your audience: Engaging with your audience is essential to building a loyal following on LinkedIn. Respond to comments on your posts, ask questions, and start conversations with your followers. Make sure that your responses are thoughtful and add value to the conversation. Encourage your followers to share their own experiences and opinions, and acknowledge and thank them for their contributions.
- Leverage LinkedIn groups: LinkedIn groups can be a powerful way to reach new audiences and build engagement with your content. Find relevant groups in your niche and join them. Participate in conversations, share your content, and connect with other members. Make sure that ***you're adding value to the group and not just promoting your own content.*** Consider starting your own group around a specific topic or interest within your niche.
- Collaborate with other LinkedIn influencers: Collaborating with other LinkedIn influencers can effectively expand your reach and build engagement with your content. Look for influencers in your niche with a similar target audience and approach them with a collaboration proposal. You might suggest guest posting on each other's profiles, hosting a joint webinar or podcast, or co-creating content. By working with other influencers, you'll be able to leverage their audiences and build your own following more quickly.
- Use LinkedIn ads: LinkedIn ads can be a powerful way to reach new audiences and promote your content to a wider audience. Consider using sponsored content ads, sponsored InMail, or text ads to target specific demographics or job titles in your niche. Ensure your ads are high-quality and relevant to your target audience and include a clear call-to-action to encourage engagement and conversions.
- Analyze your performance: Finally, it's important to regularly analyze your performance on LinkedIn to identify what's working and what's not. Use LinkedIn's built-in analytics tools to track your follower growth, engagement rates, and content performance. Look for trends

and patterns in your data, and use these insights to refine your content strategy and optimize your approach for maximum impact.

- Use hashtags: Hashtags are a powerful tool for increasing your visibility on LinkedIn. Research and use relevant hashtags in your posts to reach a wider audience and attract more followers. Use a mix of broad and specific hashtags to maximize your reach and engagement.
- Analyze your metrics: Monitoring your metrics is essential to understanding what content resonates with your audience and how to improve your strategy. Use LinkedIn's analytics tool to track your engagement, reach, and follower growth. Pay attention to which posts perform best and adjust your strategy accordingly.
- Continuously improve: Building a large, active LinkedIn following takes time and effort. Continuously analyze your metrics, experiment with new content formats, and engage with your followers to refine your strategy and maximize your passive income potential. Stay up-to-date with your industry or niche's latest trends and best practices, and adjust your strategy accordingly.

By following these steps, you can build a large and engaged following on LinkedIn and maximize your potential for passive income opportunities. Remember that building a following takes time and effort, but consistently providing value to your followers' feed accelerates the process.

Here's a checklist for building a large and engaged LinkedIn following for maximum passive income:

- **Optimize your profile**: Ensure your LinkedIn profile is complete, up-to-date, and optimized with relevant keywords.
- **Create quality content:** Develop a content strategy and create high-quality, engaging content that provides value to your target audience.
- **Engage with your audience:** Respond to comments and messages from your followers and engage with their content.
- **Join LinkedIn groups:** Join and participate in relevant LinkedIn groups to connect with like-minded individuals and expand your network.

- **Utilize LinkedIn Live:** Use LinkedIn Live to host live events and webinars.
- **Collaborate with others:** Partner with other LinkedIn influencers or brands to cross-promote content and reach new audiences.
- **Utilize LinkedIn Ads:** Consider running LinkedIn Ads to promote your content and reach a wider audience.
- **Analyze your performance:** Use LinkedIn Analytics to track your performance and identify what's working and what's not.
- **Stay up-to-date with trends:** Keep up with the latest LinkedIn trends and algorithms to stay relevant.
- **Be patient and persistent:** Building a substantial and engaged following on LinkedIn takes time and effort. Stay patient and persistent, and continue to provide value to your audience.

Insight into Successful Professional Relations:

"Contribute as much as you can, add value, and help others selflessly."

The essence of building meaningful professional relations lies in selfless contribution and genuine value addition. Shift away from transactional approaches and focus on creating relationships that stand the test of time.

Embark on this journey armed with these strategies, and witness your LinkedIn presence transform into a thriving hub for passive income opportunities.

Hacks for Building a Large and Engaged LinkedIn Following

Hack-1: LinkedIn News Engagement

Strategy:

- Follow LinkedIn News Pages: Identify and follow the LinkedIn News page specific to your country.
- Daily Engagement: Regularly visit the LinkedIn News page, read articles, and actively engage by generating comments on posts from industry experts.

- Relationship Building: Take the next 3 months to consistently comment, appreciate, and engage with experts. Observe the impact on your visibility over time.

Benefits:

- Enhanced Visibility: Active engagement on the LinkedIn News page boosts your visibility within the professional community.
- Relationship Building: Establishing connections and building relationships with industry experts.

Execution: Consistent daily engagement for three months and observe the enhancement in visibility and connections.

Hack-2: Virtual or In-person Meetings

Strategy:

- Accept Every Connection Request: Accept all connection requests on LinkedIn.
- Schedule Appointments: Within 1 to 3 months of connecting, schedule virtual or in-person meetings.
- Casual Discussions: Use these meetings for casual discussions, introductions, and understanding each other's values and thought processes.

Benefits:

- Strengthen Connections: Personalized meetings strengthen connections beyond the digital realm.
- Understanding Values: In-depth understanding of the values and thought processes of your connections.

Execution: Foster meaningful connections beyond the digital realm, allowing for deeper understanding and relationship building.

Hack-3: Building Mastermind Communities

Strategy:

- Identify Like-minded Individuals: Find individuals with similar interests and goals on LinkedIn.
- Create a Community: Establish a mastermind community or join existing ones.
- Collaborative Learning: Engage in collaborative learning and idea exchange within the community.

Benefits:

- Collective Knowledge: Tap into the collective knowledge of like-minded individuals.
- Collaborative Opportunities: Opportunities for collaboration and joint ventures may arise.

Execution: Create an environment where collective expertise nurtures growth, ideation, and mutual benefit.

Next Chapter: "Monetizing Your LinkedIn Following: Strategies for Success in 2024"

Chapter 6

Monetizing Your LinkedIn Following: Strategies for Success in 2024

"Value fuels income. Give to your network, create endless opportunities."-Amit Dubey

Monetizing your LinkedIn following can be a great way to earn passive income in 2024. Here are some strategies for successfully monetizing your LinkedIn following:

- **Use sponsored content and Affiliate Marketing:** Affiliate marketing is a way to earn a commission by promoting other people's products. You can share affiliate links in your LinkedIn posts or create sponsored content for brands. But Before you start monetizing your LinkedIn following, defining your niche is important. This will help you create content that resonates with your audience and build a following genuinely interested in what you offer. And last but not least, work with brands that align with your values and promote products or services that you genuinely believe in. Be transparent with your audience about sponsored content and affiliate links.
- **Selling digital products:** Create and sell digital products like eBooks, courses, or templates related to your niche. You can promote these products to your LinkedIn following and sell them on your website or other platforms. And you need a strong following on LinkedIn to

monetize your profile. Engage with your audience by posting regularly, responding to comments, and sharing valuable content. You can also promote your profile on other social media platforms or through email marketing.

- **Coaching or Consulting:** If you have expertise in a particular area, you can offer coaching or consulting services to your LinkedIn following. Use your LinkedIn profile to promote your services and share success stories to attract clients. Create content that provides value to your audience. Share your knowledge and expertise in your niche and offer practical tips and advice. This will help you build trust with your audience and establish yourself as an authority in your niche.
- **Sponsored Posts:** Brands always seek influencers to help promote their products. If you have a large and engaged following on LinkedIn, you can partner with brands to create sponsored content that promotes their products or services.
- **Host Webinars or Speaking Engagements:** If you have established yourself as an authority in your niche, you can offer speaking engagements or presentations to companies or organizations in your industry. Use LinkedIn to showcase your speaking experience and promote your services.
- **Create a Membership Site:** Create a membership site that offers exclusive content or access to a community for a fee. Use LinkedIn to promote your membership site and attract new members.
- **Provide Product Reviews:** Share your honest reviews of products related to your niche on your LinkedIn profile. You can monetize this by including affiliate links or sponsored content in your posts.
- **Advertising:** If you have a large following on LinkedIn, you can consider selling advertising space on your profile or in your content.
- **Crowdfunding:** If you have an innovative product or idea related to your niche, you can use crowdfunding platforms to raise funds from your LinkedIn following.
- **E-Commerce:** If you have a physical product to sell, you can create an e-commerce store and promote it to your LinkedIn following.

In order to successfully monetize your LinkedIn following, it's important to provide value to your audience, build trust, and establish yourself as an authority in your niche. It's also important to be transparent and honest with your audience about any sponsored content or affiliate links.

Additionally, it's important to diversify your income streams and not rely solely on one strategy. Test different strategies and see what works best for you and your audience.

Remember, building a successful passive income stream on LinkedIn takes time and effort, but it is possible to achieve financial freedom with the right strategies and persistence.

Here's a checklist for this chapter on "Monetizing Your LinkedIn Following: Strategies for Success in 2024":

- Identify your niche and target audience
- Create high-quality content that resonates with your audience
- Grow your following by engaging with your audience and using relevant hashtags
- Build relationships with brands and businesses that align with your niche
- Explore different monetization strategies such as sponsored posts, affiliate marketing, and creating digital products/services
- Use analytics tools to track your performance and make data-driven decisions
- Continuously test and adjust your monetization strategies to optimize your results
- Stay up-to-date with trends and changes in the LinkedIn algorithm and adjust your strategy accordingly
- Prioritize authenticity and transparency in your monetization efforts to build trust with your audience
- Have patience and persistence - building a profitable LinkedIn following takes time and effort.

Hack:

Absolutely, becoming a LinkedIn Learning instructor can significantly boost your authority and credibility within your niche. Creating a course that directly addresses your audience's needs and challenges is an excellent way to establish expertise. Additionally, the royalties earned based on your course's performance provide a valuable passive income stream.

The next chapter, "Leveraging LinkedIn Growth Hack tool BRIALO for Passive Income in 2024," promises to unravel cutting-edge strategies that leverage the power of BRIALO to maximize passive income on LinkedIn.

Chapter 7

Leveraging LinkedIn Growth Hack tool BRIALO for Passive Income in 2024

"Turn your LinkedIn connections into opportunities with BRIALO's brilliance."-Amit Dubey

You will relate to this part if you've ever found yourself staring at a blank screen, pondering what to post on LinkedIn. Ready to elevate your LinkedIn game? Let me introduce you to BRIALO, the game-changer you've been waiting for.

What is BRIALO?

In the vast landscape of LinkedIn, where content is king, BRIALO emerges as a powerful ally. It's not just a tool; it's the secret sauce that can transform your content creation woes into a seamless, engaging experience. BRIALO, short for **Brilliant LinkedIn Operations,** is an intuitive platform designed to unlock the true potential of LinkedIn, offering a suite of features to elevate your content strategy and lead generation efforts.

Why BRIALO Matters:

Ever felt the pressure of constantly generating compelling content for your LinkedIn audience? Wondered if there's a way to consistently stay on top of your game? BRIALO is the answer, providing a holistic solution to your content creation and lead generation needs.

Features of BRIALO:

1 Content Ideas on Demand:

- Creator's Block? No More! BRIALO is your go-to muse, generating tailored content ideas for your industry and audience. Keep your LinkedIn content fresh and engaging effortlessly.

2 Captivating LinkedIn Posts:

- Stand Out in the Feed! Craft attention-grabbing posts that resonate with your audience, boosting visibility and establishing your thought leadership for a robust personal brand.

3 Irresistible Hooks:

- Capture Attention! BRIALO helps you create compelling hooks that keep your audience hooked to every word. Drive more engagement and make your content go viral.

4 Growth Tracking:

- Fine-tune Your Strategy! Stay in the know about what's working and what's not. BRIALO provides insights to optimize your personal branding strategy for maximum impact.

For Whom is BRIALO?

1 Busy Professionals:

- Time is of the essence. BRIALO is designed for professionals juggling multiple tasks, providing a streamlined solution for LinkedIn growth.

2 Consultants:

- Boost Your Consulting Business. BRIALO is tailor-made for busy consultants seeking effective LinkedIn strategies.

3 CEOs:

- Lead Your Industry. Busy CEOs can leverage BRIALO to enhance their LinkedIn presence and connect with a broader audience.

4 Freelancers:

- Maximize Freelance Opportunities. BRIALO is a valuable asset for freelancers seeking authentic lead generation and network expansion.

Why BRIALO for Your Growth?

1 Endless Content Ideas:

- Beat Creative Slumps. Generate a plethora of post ideas tailored to your industry and audience. Say goodbye to content block.

2 Effortless Post Creation:

- No More Writer's Block. Easily craft captivating posts and boost your visibility to become a recognized thought leader.

3 Scroll-Stopper Hooks:

- Rise Above the Noise Supercharge engagement with attention-grabbing hooks that make your content stand out in the bustling LinkedIn feed.

4 Find Active LinkedIn Members and integrate in CRM:

- Efficient Management. Use BRIALO's unique Chrome extension (https://chromewebstore.google.com/detail/brialo-openai-gpt-linkedi/jmapgdmcamlapgpedipfadnjbjofffle) that scraps any LinkedIn post to find active members to add them to your network.

5 Personalized Connect Requests

- Build Meaningful Connections. Send personalized connect requests, enhancing your chances of building authentic relationships.

How to Unleash BRIALO Magic:

Visit getbrialo.io and Explore Each Feature.

Ready to transform your LinkedIn presence and supercharge your passive income journey? BRIALO is the magic wand you've been searching for—your guide to conquering the LinkedIn realm with ease. Unleash the power of BRIALO and watch your LinkedIn strategy reach new heights!

Here's a checklist summarizing the key action points from the BRIALO chapter:

1 Explore BRIALO Features:
   - Visit [BRIALO's website](https://getbrialo.io/) to understand and explore all the features.

2 Generate Content Ideas:
   - Use BRIALO to generate content ideas tailored to your industry and audience.
   - Ensure your LinkedIn content stays fresh and engaging.

3 Create and Schedule Posts:
   - Leverage BRIALO to create captivating posts that resonate with your target audience.
   - Schedule posts to maintain a consistent presence on LinkedIn.

4 Utilize Hook Generator:
   - Enhance engagement by crafting compelling hooks with BRIALO.
   - Keep your audience hooked with attention-grabbing introductions.

5 Track Your Growth:
   - Regularly monitor the performance of your LinkedIn strategy using BRIALO analytics.
   - Fine-tune your approach based on insights for maximum impact.

6 For Whom BRIALO is Designed:
   - Recognize that BRIALO is designed for busy professionals, consultants, CEOs, and freelancers.

7 Maximize Content Ideas:
   - Utilize BRIALO to never run out of ideas for LinkedIn content.
   - Generate hundreds of post ideas, ensuring a constant stream of captivating content.

8 Effortlessly Write LinkedIn Posts:
   - Use BRIALO to overcome writer's block and effortlessly craft attention-grabbing LinkedIn posts.
   - Boost visibility and establish yourself as a thought leader in your field.

9 Create Scroll Stopper Hooks:
   - Supercharge engagement by creating attention-grabbing hooks with BRIALO.
   - Stand out in the LinkedIn feed and keep your connections coming back for more.

10 Utilize CRM Features:
   - Leverage BRIALO's CRM functionality for efficient management of your LinkedIn connections.
   - Extract active users' email IDs and send personalized connect requests.

Implementing these points will help you harness the power of **BRIALO** for your LinkedIn strategy.

#Next Chapter: Networking on LinkedIn: Building Connections for Passive Income Opportunities.

Chapter 8

Networking on LinkedIn: Building Connections for Passive Income Opportunities

"Don't wait. The time will never be just right."
-Napoleon Hill

Networking on LinkedIn is essential to building a strong personal brand and maximizing your passive income opportunities. In this chapter, we will discuss how to network effectively on LinkedIn in 2024 and how to use your connections to generate passive income streams.

Optimize Your LinkedIn Profile

Before you start networking on LinkedIn, you must ensure your LinkedIn profile is complete and optimized. This means having a professional headshot, a compelling headline, and a detailed summary that showcases your skills, experience, and achievements. You should also include relevant keywords throughout your profile to make it easier for people to find you on the platform.

Identify Your Target Audience

To network effectively on LinkedIn, you must understand your target audience clearly. This includes identifying the industries, job titles, and companies most relevant to your niche. You can use LinkedIn's search function and filters to find people who fit your target audience criteria and start connecting with them.

Connect Strategically

When connecting with people on LinkedIn, it's essential to do so strategically. Don't just connect with everyone you come across; instead, focus on connecting with people who are relevant to your niche and can help you achieve your passive income goals. When sending connection requests, be sure to personalize your message and explain why you want to connect

Build Relationships

Networking is all about building relationships, and LinkedIn is no exception. Once you've connected with someone, take the time to get to know them and build a rapport. This means engaging with their content, commenting on their posts, and sharing useful information or insights with them. You should also be willing to offer value to your connections and help them achieve their goals, whether that's through sharing your expertise or introducing them to other relevant people in your network.

Join LinkedIn Groups

LinkedIn groups are a great way to connect with like-minded individuals in your niche and expand your network. Look for groups that are relevant to your niche and join them. Once you're a member, engage with the group by asking questions, offering insights, and sharing useful resources. You can also use groups to connect with other members and build relationships that can lead to passive income opportunities.

Attend LinkedIn Events

LinkedIn also hosts events, both in-person and virtual, that are designed to help professionals network and connect with each other. Look for events that are relevant to your niche and attend them. This is an excellent opportunity to meet new people, build relationships, and potentially find passive income opportunities.

Leverage Your Network

Finally, once you've built a strong network on LinkedIn, you can leverage it to generate passive income opportunities. This can include promoting your products or services to your connections, partnering with other professionals in your niche, or even launching a joint venture. The key is to use your network strategically and be willing to offer value in return.

In conclusion, networking on LinkedIn is a powerful tool for building your personal brand and generating passive income opportunities. By optimizing your profile, identifying your target audience, connecting strategically, building relationships, joining groups, attending events, and leveraging your network, you can establish yourself as a thought leader in your niche and achieve your passive income goals.

Here's a short checklist for "Networking on LinkedIn: Building Connections for Passive Income Opportunities":

Define your target audience and the type of connections you want to make.

- Optimize your LinkedIn profile to make it attractive to potential connections.
- Actively search for and connect with people in your target audience.
- Engage with your connections by liking, commenting, and sharing their content.
- Participate in LinkedIn groups related to your niche to expand your network and build credibility.
- Attend virtual networking events and webinars to meet new connections and strengthen existing relationships.

- Use personalized messages to initiate conversations and build meaningful relationships with your connections.
- Offer value to your connections by sharing helpful content, making introductions, and providing insights.
- Nurture your connections by staying in touch, checking in, and following up on opportunities.
- Continuously evaluate and refine your networking strategy to maximize your passive income potential on LinkedIn.

This chapter explores the pivotal role of networking on LinkedIn for cultivating passive income in 2024. It details strategies for optimizing profiles, strategically connecting, and leveraging networks. By emphasizing profile optimization, strategic connections, relationship-building, group engagement, event participation, and leveraging connections for passive income, this chapter guides readers toward maximizing their LinkedIn potential for lucrative passive income opportunities.

Next Chapter: "Outsourcing Techniques for Streamlining Your LinkedIn Passive Income"

Chapter 9

Outsourcing Techniques for Streamlining Your LinkedIn Passive Income

"Outsource wisely, unlock time for meaningful connections, and watch your LinkedIn income thrive."-Amit Dubey

In the ever-evolving landscape of online business and passive income generation, the strategic use of outsourcing has become a game-changer. This chapter delves into the intricacies of outsourcing techniques tailored to streamline the process of generating passive income on LinkedIn in 2024.

Understanding LinkedIn Outreach:

LinkedIn outreach is a strategic approach to connect, engage, and build relationships with potential clients, collaborators, or prospects on the LinkedIn platform. It involves reaching out to individuals or businesses relevant to your niche with the goal of fostering meaningful connections that may lead to passive income opportunities.

Reaching Clients on LinkedIn:

Reaching clients on LinkedIn involves a thoughtful and personalized approach. Start by optimizing your LinkedIn profile to showcase your expertise and value proposition clearly. Identify your target audience and use advanced search filters to find potential clients. Craft personalized connection requests, highlighting mutual interests or commonalities, and expressing genuine interest in connecting.

Tips for Successful LinkedIn Outreach:

1 **Profile Optimization:** Before initiating outreach, ensure your profile reflects your expertise and the value you bring. A compelling profile is more likely to attract positive attention.

2 **Targeted Connection Requests:** Be strategic in sending connection requests. Tailor your messages to explain why you want to connect and how it can be mutually beneficial.

3 **Engagement Strategy**: After connecting, engage with your network's content. Like, comment, and share posts to stay on their radar and build rapport.

4 **Personalized Messaging:** When reaching out for potential collaboration or business opportunities, always personalize your messages. Clearly state the value you bring and how it aligns with their goals.

Sample of Personaolized connection Request:

1 Hi Daksh,

Vrinda Gupta's post on the Linkfluence Creator Summit caught my eye, and I'm all in on LinkedIn's potential for creators. As a fellow enthusiast, let's connect. Your insights could be the key to leveling up our LinkedIn game. Excited to chat about the summit!

Best,

Amit Dubey

2 Hi Aadish,

I came across your role in the Tedx organizer team. As a dedicated youth empowerment keynote speaker, I'd love to connect and discuss how I can contribute to the success of your events.

Best,

Amit Dubey

3 Hi Kunle,

I am searching for the top executive network in the consulting industry. I would like to connect with you on this platform and expand our network.

Regards

Amit Dubey

Vectors Group

4 Hey Amit,

Came across your profile.

Love what you're working on.

Just reaching out to connect.

Cheers!

Jason

5 Hi Anusha,

I am searching for the top executive network in the consulting industry. I would like to connect with you on this platform and expand our network.

Regards

Amit Dubey

Vectors Group

5 **Consistent Follow-Up:** Effective outreach involves consistent follow-up. Don't be afraid to follow up with a personalized message if your initial connection request or message doesn't receive a response. You also check their post and comment on the post.

LinkedIn Outreach: The Art of Building Connections.

Successful LinkedIn outreach goes beyond mere connection requests. It involves building authentic relationships that can evolve into fruitful opportunities. Tailoring your approach, personalizing your interactions, and strategically outsourcing certain tasks can significantly enhance your LinkedIn passive income endeavors.

Next Chapter: "Scaling Your LinkedIn Passive Income Business: Taking it to the Next Level in 2024

Chapter 10

Scaling Your LinkedIn Passive Income Business: Taking it to the Next Level in 2024

Congratulations on successfully establishing a passive income business on LinkedIn! The journey so far has been rewarding, and now it's time to explore strategies that will propel your business to new heights in 2024. Scaling your LinkedIn passive income business requires thoughtful planning and strategic execution. Let's delve into key strategies that will contribute to your business's growth and success.

Diversify Your Income Streams

While your current LinkedIn passive income streams have provided a stable foundation, diversification is a crucial step for long-term success. Explore additional passive income opportunities within your niche. This could involve affiliate marketing, creating and selling e-books, developing courses, or even launching your own products or services. Diversification not only enhances stability but also opens up new revenue channels.

Example: If your passive income primarily comes from sponsored content, consider launching an e-book that delves deeper into your expertise. This not only provides an additional revenue stream but also positions you as an authority in your field.

Outsource or Delegate Tasks

As your business expands, so will your workload. To manage this effectively, consider outsourcing or delegating tasks. Virtual assistants, freelancers, or contractors can handle routine responsibilities, allowing you to focus on strategic and high-impact tasks that drive growth.

Example: If managing your content schedule becomes overwhelming, hiring a virtual assistant to handle posting and engagement can free up your time for more significant aspects of your business.

Expand Your Network

Networking is a continuous process. Actively seek opportunities to connect with professionals in your industry. Attend events, both online and offline, to broaden your network. Engage with your existing connections, share valuable insights, and nurture relationships. A robust network not only fosters collaboration but also expands your business's reach.

Example: Collaborate with individuals in complementary niches to cross-promote content. This expands your audience and introduces your business to new, relevant circles.

Automate Your Processes

Efficiency is key to scalability. Automate repetitive tasks using tools and software. Content scheduling, email marketing, and social media management can be streamlined, saving time and ensuring consistency.

Example: Use social media management tools to schedule posts in advance, ensuring a consistent and timely presence on LinkedIn without manual daily intervention.

Set Clear Goals and Benchmarks

To scale effectively, establish clear goals and benchmarks for growth. Define key performance indicators (KPIs) relevant to your business. Regularly assess your progress to ensure alignment with your objectives.

Example: If your goal is to increase passive income by a certain percentage, set specific quarterly targets. Regularly review financial metrics to gauge performance against these targets.

Invest in Your Business

Consider strategic investments to facilitate growth. This could involve increased advertising efforts, upgraded technology, or hiring additional staff. Invest wisely to support the evolving needs of your expanding business.

Example: Allocate a budget for targeted advertising campaigns on LinkedIn to reach a broader audience and attract potential collaborators or clients.

Continuously Improve Your Skills and Knowledge

Stay ahead in your industry by continuously improving your skills and knowledge. Attend relevant conferences, enroll in courses, read industry publications, and engage with other professionals. This ongoing learning ensures you remain at the forefront of your niche.

Example: Dedicate time each month to learning about emerging trends in your industry. Apply this knowledge to refine your content strategy and maintain relevance.

In conclusion, scaling your LinkedIn passive income business is a dynamic process that requires dedication and strategic decision-making. By diversifying income streams, outsourcing tasks, expanding your network, automating processes, setting clear goals, making strategic investments, and staying informed, you position your business for sustained growth in 2024 and beyond.

"LinkedIn Passive Income 2024: A Practical Guide" is a comprehensive and actionable guide for individuals who want to earn passive income through the LinkedIn platform. This book is filled with insights, strategies, and practical tips that will enable readers to leverage the power of LinkedIn to create a passive income stream.

Navigating Deep into Lucrative Passive Income Streams in 2024.

In the dynamic world of passive income, the year 2024 unfolds a plethora of opportunities, catering to diverse interests and skill sets. These income avenues not only promise ease of initiation but also exhibit the potential for scalability, making them accessible for individuals seeking financial independence. Let's embark on a detailed exploration of each passive income stream, considering crucial factors such as the ease of starting, initial capital requirements, and scalability potential.

1. Start a YouTube Channel:

YouTube stands as an ever-growing platform for content creators to transform their passion into a source of income. Initiating a YouTube channel is moderately easy, demanding consistent content creation, proficiency with video editing tools, and a camera setup. The capital requirements are relatively low, with basic recording equipment and software for editing. The scalability of a YouTube channel is high, tied directly to the growth in subscribers and views. As the channel gains popularity, monetization avenues through ads and sponsorships amplify. Payments, initially around $500 per month, can significantly escalate with substantial growth, potentially reaching thousands of dollars monthly.

2. Write a Book:

For those with a penchant for storytelling or possessing expertise in a particular domain, writing a book can be a fulfilling and sustainable passive income source. The ease of initiation varies, depending on one's writing skills and the complexity of the chosen subject. Capital requirements are generally low to moderate, covering expenses such as cover design, editing, and marketing. Scalability is moderate and contingent upon book sales, yet adaptations into different formats, translations, and audiobook versions contribute to additional revenue streams. Payment outcomes for self-published authors typically range between $1,000 and $5,000 per book annually.

3. Join the Amazon Affiliate Program:

Affiliate marketing through platforms like Amazon provides a straightforward entry into the realm of passive income. The initiation process is highly accessible, involving a simple registration process and the promotion of products through affiliate links. Capital requirements are notably low, as affiliates don't need to deal with inventory or product creation. The scalability of the Amazon Affiliate Program is moderate and closely tied to the quality of content produced and the reach of the audience. Initial payments might range from $100 to $500 per month and can grow substantially with increased conversions and expanded audience engagement.

4. Create an Online Course:

Sharing expertise through online courses has become a lucrative venture, particularly with the rising demand for skill development. The ease of initiation is moderate, demanding proficiency in a specific subject and an understanding of effective teaching methods. Capital requirements are generally low to moderate, covering expenses such as platform fees, basic course creation tools, and marketing. The scalability potential is high, contingent on the quality of the course and effective promotional efforts. Earnings from online courses can range widely, from $1,000 to $10,000 monthly, depending on the course's popularity and the instructor's marketing strategies.

5. Start Niche Blogging:

Niche blogging provides a platform for individuals passionate about specific topics to share their knowledge and insights. Initiating a niche blog is moderately easy, requiring content creation skills, a basic understanding of website setup, and the ability to produce engaging content. Capital requirements are low to moderate, covering expenses such as domain registration, hosting fees, and potentially, content creation tools. Scalability is high, with income growing as blog traffic increases through consistent, quality content. Initial earnings may range from $500 to $1,000 per month, scaling up to $5,000 or more with a substantial and engaged audience.

6. Market a Niche Affiliate Opportunity:

This avenue involves marketing specific products or services within a niche, offering an accessible entry point for those with a genuine interest in the promoted items. The ease of initiation is moderate, requiring an understanding of and enthusiasm for the products being promoted. Capital requirements are low, as there is no need for inventory or product creation. Scalability ranges from moderate to high, depending on the affiliate program's structure and the level of engagement with the target audience. Initial payments could start at $100 to $500 monthly and have the potential to scale up significantly with increased referrals and conversions.

7. No-Code Software: Premium Business Model and Recurring Revenue:

Venturing into the realm of no-code software development provides a premium business model with recurring revenue potential. The initiation process is moderately easy, demanding familiarity with no-code platforms and a creative approach to problem-solving. Capital requirements are low to moderate, covering initial development costs and subscription tools for no-code platforms. Scalability is high, with revenue increasing as the user base grows and subscriptions renew. Initial earnings might range from $500 to $1,000 monthly, scaling up significantly with a growing and loyal user base.

The passive income landscape in 2024 is rich with opportunities catering to varied interests and skill sets. Each avenue has its unique characteristics, making them suitable for different individuals. Success in these endeavors demands dedication, continuous improvement, and adaptability to market trends. As individuals embark on their passive income journey, exploring these avenues can open doors to financial autonomy and a more fulfilling lifestyle.

The book is divided into ten chapters, each of which provides readers with specific insights and actionable steps for building a strong LinkedIn profile, identifying and targeting profitable niches, creating content that drives passive income, building a large and engaged following, monetizing their LinkedIn following, leveraging LinkedIn ads, networking for passive income opportunities, and automating and outsourcing techniques.

In the first chapter, readers are ***introduced to the concept of passive income on LinkedIn*** and given an overview of the niche in 2024. This chapter provides a solid foundation for the rest of the book by giving readers a clear understanding of what they can expect and what they need to do to get started.

Chapter two focuses on ***building a strong LinkedIn profile to attract passive income opportunities.*** This chapter provides readers with step-by-step instructions for optimizing their profile, including crafting a compelling headline, writing a strong summary, and highlighting their skills and achievements.

Chapter three provides readers with insights into ***identifying and targeting profitable LinkedIn niches in 2024.*** This chapter teaches readers how to conduct market research, identify opportunities, and choose a niche that is right for them.

Chapter four focuses on ***creating content that drives passive income on LinkedIn.*** This chapter provides readers with strategies for creating high-quality content that resonates with their audience and drives engagement.

Chapter five is all about ***amplifying Influence – The Roadmap to a Thriving LinkedIn Following for Passive Income.*** This chapter gives readers insights into how to grow their following, including techniques for engaging with their audience and leveraging LinkedIn groups.

Chapter six provides readers with ***insights into monetizing their LinkedIn following.*** This chapter teaches readers how to create and promote products and services that will appeal to their audience and generate passive income.

Chapter seven focuses on ***Leveraging the LinkedIn Growth Hack tool BRIALO for Passive Income in 2024.*** This chapter provides readers with step-by-step instructions for creating effective LinkedIn ad campaigns and maximizing their return on investment.

Chapter eight is all about ***networking on LinkedIn for passive income opportunities.*** This chapter teaches readers how to build relationships with potential clients and partners and leverage LinkedIn for lead generation and business development.

Chapter nine focuses on ***outsourcing techniques for streamlining their LinkedIn passive income business.*** This chapter provides readers with insights into how to automate and outsource tasks, freeing up their time to focus on the core aspects of their business.

Finally, chapter ten provides readers with ***strategies for scaling their LinkedIn passive income business to the next level in 2024.*** This chapter teaches readers how to set goals, measure their progress, and develop a long-term strategy for growth and success.

In summary, "LinkedIn Passive Income 2024: A Practical Guide" is a comprehensive and actionable guide for anyone who wants to earn passive income through LinkedIn. The book provides readers with step-by-step instructions for building a strong LinkedIn profile, identifying profitable niches, creating engaging content, building a large and engaged following, monetizing their audience, leveraging LinkedIn ads, networking for opportunities, automating and outsourcing tasks, and scaling their business. With this book as a guide, readers will be well-equipped to succeed in the world of LinkedIn passive income in 2024 and beyond.

12 LinkedIn Profile Tips

Tip #1: LinkedIn Profile Funnel

Photo, Cover, and Headline

AWARENESS (HEADLINE, LINKEDIN PHOTO, AND COVER PHOTO)

Goal: It's your elevator pitch, so you need to show who you are and what you do as clear as possible, so people will want to click on your profile to check more information

CONSIDERATION (SUMMARY, EXPERIENCE)

Goal: Here you have a lot of space to share details, for example: • describe how exactly you solve client's pains, • what's something unique in your approach or company, • what were your results.

DECISION (MEDIA, CTA AT THE END OF DESCRIPTION)

Goal: You Now people know who you're, what you do, and how exactly you can help them. They just need to go to the correct place to start talking to your company

So, your goal here is to let people easily: • book a demo with you, • check your blog, • write an email to you.

So now we understand the goal of each part of the LinkedIn profile, so we can go through each of those blocks and make them better

Tip #2: LinkedIn Profile Photo

Tip #3: Cover/Background Photo

Tip #4: Headline

Tip #5: Summary.

Tip #6: Media

Tip #7: Customize LinkedIn profile URL

Tip #8: Experience

Tip #9: Skills

Tip #10: Articles

Tip #11: LinkedIn Profile SEO

Tip #12: Create content

The Comprehensive 2024 LinkedIn Marketing Handbook: Optimal Image + Video Dimensions and Beyond!

Recommended Image Sizes for LinkedIn Ads

- Sponsored posts: 1200 x 627 pixels
- Sponsored InMail: 300 x 250 pixels
- Text ads: 100 x 100 pixels
- Carousel ads: 1080 x 1080 pixels
- Video ads: landscape (1920 x 1080 pixels), square (1080 x 1080 pixels), and vertical (1080 x 1920 pixels).

LinkedIn Post Images

- Web links: 1200×627 pixels
- Carousel post: 1920 x 1080 or 1080 x 1080
- Maximum video length: 10 minutes

LinkedIn Profiles

LinkedIn's recommended image sizes for your profile are:

- Best LinkedIn profile picture size: 400 x 400 pixels
- Background image size: 1584 x 396 pixels

LinkedIn Company Pages

- Company logo size: 300 x 300 pixels
- Square image: 60 x 60 pixels
- Cover photo size: 1128 x 191 pixels

LinkedIn Groups

- Logo size: 300 x 300
- Banner image size: 1536 x 768

LinkedIn Background Banner

- LinkedIn background banner, or cover image: 1536 x 768.

Best Video Sizes for LinkedIn

- LinkedIn video size: 256 x 144 (minimum) to 4096 x 2304 (maximum)
- Video file size: 75KB to a maximum of 5GB
- LinkedIn video duration: A maximum of 15 minutes when uploading from desktop and 10 minutes when uploading from LinkedIn's mobile app
- Frame rates: 10fps - 60 fps
- Bit rates: 192 kbps - 30 Mbps

All sizes are in pixels.

LinkedIn personal profiles, optimum image sizes

- LinkedIn profile picture size: 400 x 400
- LinkedIn banner or background photo size: 1584 x 396

LinkedIn company pages, optimum image sizes

- LinkedIn company logo size: 300 x 300
- LinkedIn banner / cover photo size: 1128 x 191

LinkedIn posts, optimum image sizes

- LinkedIn post single or multi-image: 1080 x 1080 (square) 1920 x 1080 (portrait)
- LinkedIn article featured image: 1200 x 644
- LinkedIn article banner image: 600 x 322
- LinkedIn image sizes for blog post link images: 1200 x 627
- LinkedIn carousel post: 1080 x 1080 OR 1920 x 1080
- LinkedIn carousel best format: PDF
- LinkedIn video size: 256 x 144 (minimum) to 4096 x 2304 (maximum)
- LinkedIn video file size: 75KB to 200MB
- Maximum LinkedIn video length: 10 minutes
- LinkedIn Stories image size: 1080 x 1920

LinkedIn Events, optimum image sizes

- LinkedIn event logo size: 300 x 300 - square
- LinkedIn event 'banner' size: 16:9 ratio so 1600 x 900 pixels works

LinkedIn Groups, optimum image sizes

- LinkedIn groups logo size: 300 x 300
- LinkedIn groups banner size: 1536 x 768

List of AI-based Tools for Seamless Content Creation on LinkedIn

Here's a list of AI-related tools and technologies that can be beneficial for content creation across different platforms, including LinkedIn:

BRIALO For Hassle-free content generation:

As discussed in the previous chapters, BRIALO is the tool of choice of content creation on LinkedIn for busy professionals and creators alike.

Canva with AI Elements:

Canva has started integrating AI elements into its platform, allowing for easier image editing, design suggestions, and other AI-driven features to enhance visual content.

Grammarly:

While not exclusively an AI tool, Grammarly utilizes AI algorithms to provide grammar and style suggestions, helping you improve the quality of your written content on LinkedIn.

Vidyard:

Vidyard is a video platform that uses AI to provide analytics and insights into how your video content is performing. This can help you tailor your video strategy for LinkedIn.

Crystal:

Crystal uses AI to analyze public data and provide insights into personality types. This can be useful for tailoring your messaging to different audiences on LinkedIn.

Ceralytics:

Ceralytics uses AI to analyze content performance and audience engagement. This can help you refine your content strategy on LinkedIn based on data-driven insights.

Outwrite:

Similar to Grammarly, Outwrite is an AI-driven writing assistant that provides grammar and style suggestions to enhance the quality of your written content.

Lumen5:

Lumen5 is a video creation platform that uses AI to turn text into engaging video content. It's a useful tool for repurposing blog posts or articles into video format for LinkedIn.

Oribi:

Oribi is an AI-powered analytics tool that provides insights into website and content performance. This can be valuable for understanding how your LinkedIn-linked content is driving traffic.

CoSchedule Headline Analyzer:

While not strictly AI, CoSchedule's Headline Analyzer uses advanced algorithms to analyze your headlines for effectiveness. Crafting compelling headlines is crucial for LinkedIn content.

LinkedIn Outreach Messages Template

After Accepting the connection Request: -

Hi [Professional's Name],

Cheers for connecting! 🎉 Your expertise in [mention their field] is genuinely inspiring, and I'm thrilled to be part of your network.

Networking, to me, is like a collaborative adventure—full of selflessness and growth. I'm excited about the potential for some serious collaboration and a dash of fun along the way!

How about we schedule a virtual coffee chat? ☕ Your insights are pure gold, and I'm eager to bounce around ideas and share a laugh or two.

Thanks again for connecting—looking forward to making professional magic happen together!

Best,

[Your Full Name]

Hey [Professional's Name],

Thanks a bunch for joining my LinkedIn journey! 🚀 *Your expertise in [mention their field] has me doing a happy dance.*

Let's make networking a bit hilarious, shall we? If you were a superhero in your industry, what would your superpower be? 🦸 *I'm genuinely curious!*

Also, how about a virtual coffee chat to dissect the mysteries of our professional worlds? ☕ *Your insights are like the X-factor I've been looking for.*

Thanks for the connection—can't wait to share a laugh and some genius ideas!

Best,

[Your Full Name]

Hi [Professional's Name],

High-five for the connection! 🚀 *Your expertise in [mention their field] is like a beacon of awesomeness in my professional universe.*

I've always believed networking should come with a side of laughter, don't you think? So, here's a challenge: If you could have a superpower for work, what would it be? Flying to meetings or a telepathic PowerPoint skills boost? 😄

On a more serious note, I'd love to grab a virtual coffee and chat about collaboration. What do you say? Your insights are like hidden treasures, and I'm ready to embark on this professional adventure with a smile.

Thanks a bunch for connecting—looking forward to your superhero response!

Best,

[Your Full Name]

Hey [Professional's Name],

Thanks a ton for accepting the connection! Your [mention their field] prowess is basically legendary, and now I feel like I'm one-degree cooler by association. 😎

Networking, they say, is about selflessness and growth, but who said it can't be a bit hilarious too? So, quick question: If you could have a superpower for work-related stuff, what would it be? Personally, I'm leaning toward "instant coffee brewing."

I'd love to steal a moment of your time for a virtual chat—no pressure, just a chance to exchange insights and maybe share a chuckle or two. What do you say?

Thanks again for making my network infinitely cooler. Looking forward to connecting and cracking a few virtual jokes together!

Cheers,

[Your Full Name]

Hi [Professional's Name],

Thanks for making my LinkedIn cooler by one awesome connection—YOU! 🚀 *Your [mention their field] game is strong, and I'm here for the front-row seats.*

Networking is like a comedy show, right? So, if you could have a sitcom about your professional life, what would it be called? I'm thinking "The Chronicles of [Their Name]—Master of [Their Expertise]."

How about we schedule a virtual meeting to swap stories and maybe plot our sitcom pilot? Excited to connect and bring a bit of humor to our professional journey!

Cheers,

[Your Full Name]

Hey [Professional's Name],

High-five for accepting the connection! 🙌 Your [mention their field] brilliance is the secret sauce that just made my professional network gourmet.

Networking, they say, should be both insightful and hilarious. So, if your career had a theme song, what would it be? I'm leaning toward something epic, maybe with a touch of funk—because, well, why not?

Let's plan a virtual meet-up to chat about the serious stuff and sneak in a few laughs. Looking forward to connecting and discovering the melody of your career!

Best,

[Your Full Name]

Hey [Professional's Name],

Kudos on accepting the connection! 🌟 Your [mention their field] expertise is like the Oscar-winning performance in my professional network.

Networking can be serious, but why not turn it into a blockbuster movie? If your career were a film genre, what would it be? I'm thinking action-adventure with a plot twist—classic.

How about we schedule a virtual session to discuss our career blockbusters? Ready for some laughs and blockbuster insights?

Cheers,

[Your Full Name]

For the senior professionals you meet.

Dear [Mr. /Ms. Professional's Last Name],

It is truly an honor to connect with a seasoned professional like yourself. Your expertise in [mention their field] is a beacon of inspiration for aspiring professionals like me.

Networking, in my humble opinion, is an art, and with your experience, it's like connecting with a maestro. If your career had a tagline, what would it be? I'm envisioning something grand, like "Decades of Excellence in Every Chapter."

I would be immensely grateful for an opportunity to schedule a virtual meeting with you, where we can exchange insights and perhaps share a laugh or two. Your wisdom is unparalleled, and I look forward to the prospect of learning from it.

Thank you for gracing my professional network, and I hope to connect with you soon.

Respectfully,

[Your Full Name]

Dear [Mr. /Ms. Professional's Last Name],

Accepting my connection request is an honor, and I deeply appreciate your generosity in sharing your professional journey. Your achievements in [mention their field] speak volumes about your dedication and expertise.

Networking, as I see it, is an opportunity to learn from the seasoned sages. If you could distill your years of experience into one piece of advice and one joke, what would they be? I'm curious and ready to be enlightened and entertained.

I would be delighted to schedule a brief virtual meeting at your convenience. Your insights are invaluable, and I am eager to soak in some of your wisdom.

Thank you for connecting, and looking forward to the privilege of our future conversations.

Best regards,

[Your Full Name]

Dear [Mr. /Ms. Professional's Last Name],

I'm truly honored that you accepted my connection request. Your distinguished career in [mention their field] is not just impressive but sets a standard for excellence.

Networking, in the presence of seasoned professionals like yourself, feels like embarking on a journey with a master navigator. If your career were a compass, what direction would it point? I'm hoping for the true north of success and a bit of wit.

I would be privileged to schedule a virtual meeting with you, allowing me the opportunity to absorb some of your insights and, if you permit, share a lighthearted moment or two.

Thank you for enriching my network, and I eagerly anticipate the chance to connect more deeply.

Respectfully,

[Your Full Name]

Hi Jurgita,

Cheers for connecting! 🎉 Your expertise as a Human Resource is genuinely inspiring, and I'm thrilled to be part of your network. Networking, to me, is like a collaborative adventure—full of selflessness and growth. I'm excited about the potential for some serious collaboration and a dash of fun along the way! How about we schedule a virtual coffee chat this coming Saturday? ☕ Your insights are pure gold, and I'm eager to bounce around ideas and share a laugh or two. Thanks again for connecting—I'm looking forward to making professional magic happen together!

Best,

Amit Dubey

Hi Dev,

Cheers for connecting! 🎉 Your expertise in the Personal Brandi is genuinely inspiring, and I'm thrilled to be part of your network. Networking, to me, is like a collaborative adventure—full of selflessness and growth. I'm excited about the potential for some serious collaboration and a dash of fun along the way! How about we schedule a virtual coffee chat this coming Saturday? ☕ Your insights are pure gold, and I'm eager to bounce around ideas and share a laugh or two. Thanks again for connecting—I'm looking forward to making professional magic happen together!

Best,

Amit Dubey

Hi Dr. Garima.

Your profile caught my eye, and I couldn't resist reaching out. Your expertise in communication coaching is like the superhero cape I've been searching for in my professional journey.

Can we be LinkedIn buddies?

Cheers,

Amit Dubey

Hi [Professional's Name],

Hope this message finds you in the midst of conquering your workday! 👋 Your profile caught my eye, and I couldn't resist reaching out. Your expertise in [mention their field] is like the superhero cape I've been searching for in my professional journey.

Can we be LinkedIn buddies? 🚀 I promise I bring great memes and occasional bursts of workplace wisdom. Let's connect and turn our professional journeys into a sitcom of success!

Cheers,

[Your Full Name]

Hi [Professional's Name],

Your profile is the Beyoncé of LinkedIn—impressive! 🌟 Let's be work BFFs and conquer the professional world together. Ready for a connection?

Cheers,

[Your Full Name]

Hi [Professional's Name],

Your profile is a beacon of brilliance! 🌟 Let's be LinkedIn pals and share a laugh or two amidst the professional hustle.

Cheers,

[Your Full Name]

Hi [Professional's Name],

Your profile is like finding a golden ticket in the LinkedIn chocolate factory! 🍫🎫 Let's join forces and sprinkle a bit of humor into our professional escapades. I bring a mix of witty banter and industry insights—because why settle for just one, right?

Ready for a virtual handshake and some digital shenanigans?

Cheers,

[Your Full Name]

Dear readers,

As we come to the end of this book, I would like to take a moment to express my sincere gratitude for choosing to read and explore the world of LinkedIn passive income with me. I sincerely hope that the information and insights shared in these pages have been valuable and will help you in your journey towards building a successful passive income stream through LinkedIn.

I also want to extend my warmest wishes to each and every one of you. May you continue to learn and grow in all areas of your life and may your pursuits of passive income through LinkedIn be fruitful and fulfilling. Remember to always stay curious, persistent, and open-minded in your endeavors.

Thank you once again for your time and attention, and I wish you all the best in your future endeavors.

Sincerely,

Amit Dubey

www.ingramcontent.com/pod-product-compliance
Lightning Source LLC
LaVergne TN
LVHW091118150826
845673LV00002B/885

9798892334730